How to Survive Getting Fired— And Win!

BY JERRY COWLE
(who's done it)

Follett Publishing Company
Chicago

Designed by Karen Yops.
Edited by Susan David.

Library of Congress Cataloging in Publication Data

Cowle, Jerry, 1922–
  How to survive getting fired —and win!

    1. Vocational guidance.   2. Employees, Dismissal of.
I. Title.
HF5381.C697   650'.14   79–10187
ISBN 0–695–81135–5

Second Printing

To Betty, my dear wife, whose love
and support always sustained me

To my dear mother, who understood

To my friend, Frank Rice, a stranger
when he offered his friendship
during one of my darkest hours

Contents

Preface

The first time I was fired, I felt that my entire world had crumbled. For seventeen years, I'd moved steadily upward in my career, with never a setback. Life seemed to be one continual promotion and salary raise. I was totally unprepared to retrogress, and that was why it hurt so much. I didn't know which direction to turn, what to do, or how to act. But the human spirit is resilient, and I learned—the hard way.

I eventually found my way back into the world of employed people, but the scars remained. Twice in the following nine years, it happened to me again. Each time I was able to cope a little more easily.

Getting fired has become a commonplace event today, for many reasons. Many people will suffer through the same ordeal as long as businesses retrench or fail, as long as bosses' sons and daughters graduate from college, and as long as personalities clash.

I've written this book with the hope that it might help

you over the rough spots of your time "on the bricks." When I was fired, I was over forty, the sole support of my wife and three children. However, many of the problems encountered by a person who is fired are universal. Whether you're male or female, single or married, with just a few years of work under your belt or twenty or more, much of this time-tested advice will apply to you. Many of the situations I've run into and handled will be of interest to you, as will the opinions of persons I interviewed who are in a position to hire or to help job hunters find work. *How to Survive Getting Fired* can give you an edge toward escaping from the world of joblessness and feeling better about yourself while you're doing it.

Prologue:
Out of Work

When you're fired from your job, you look the same, breathe the same air, and still bleed when you're cut. But, imperceptibly, a metamorphosis takes place—you cross over into the world of the unemployed, a world where there seem to be no other occupants. There really are others, but they are silent and invisible, fighting their growing feelings of shame and worthlessness. They have been rejected, and no one appears to desire what they have to offer.

You walk down a busy street during the morning rush hour, and you don't seem to belong anywhere. You begin to envy people of all businesses and trades—people with occupations you never dreamed of having—because they are going to a place where they are known, are addressed by name, are given a paycheck regularly, and are cared about.

Being out of work for a long time can be very hard on a person. Immediately after the firing, there may be a surge of relief and optimism—you know your own worth. You know you have solid accomplishments and are saleable. Maybe you even turn down the first few firm offers because the salaries don't equal what you just left behind.

As the months pass, the leads may dwindle. You're no longer fresh merchandise, but stale goods with little shelf appeal. Then comes that endless day when the last lead has been pursued, the last phone call made, and the last letter written. You hit rock bottom. You cry in your spouse's or your friend's arms and tell of your fears for yourself and for your family. Now you know what love and marriage and friendship really mean.

Before long, your spirits change. You see thousands of windows in the buildings in the city, and you know that somewhere behind one of them must be a person who is hurting for the help of someone like you. The problem is to find that person, but once again it appears possible.

You go back to making phone calls, writing letters, and pounding the pavement. You remember people you haven't thought of in years. You review your past accomplishments and say to yourself, "You're a valuable person. Whoever hires you will be very lucky!"

At long last it happens. A worthwhile job appears for a worthwhile person. Sometimes it's when you least expect it. Sometimes help comes from surprising sources. This job may have nothing to do with your last one. But you are no longer the same person—you have learned a lot. Some of your friends turned out not to be friends. Some whom you had not regarded favorably turned out to be people of character and compassion. Strangers performed kindnesses with no thought of reciprocation.

So you go back into the mainstream of the working world. Now you place a greater value on the dignity of work. Now the word "friend" is reserved for those who are deserving of the accolade. Now you know your ordeal is over, but it hasn't been in vain. One who has been down on the floor of the gorge learns to appreciate the view from the ridge.

1

The Day
the Roof Fell In

You're sitting in your office, working on a deadline that's
coming up all too soon. Your career with the company
has been on a comfortable upward curve. Money and
responsibility have been forthcoming at regular inter-
vals. In other words, you belong. You're part of the
"family."

So you don't find it unusual when the phone rings
and your boss asks you to drop by. It happens several
times a week. In fact, you never really think of him as a
boss. He's your friend; it's Frank and Joe. Your wives
are friends, too.

You saunter over to Frank's office and wonder why his
secretary doesn't smile back at you. Frank is behind his
desk, looking all business. "What's happening, Frank?"
you ask breezily, flopping into his big leather chair and
casually draping your leg over the armrest. You kind of
hope he'll ask you about the report that's due on Friday.
Then you can surprise him with the good news that it's

being typed right now and should be on his desk by Wednesday.

You realize that Frank hasn't answered your question. He's sitting there, stiff and formal, holding a sheet of paper in front of his face. You wonder what in blazes can be so important as to make him act so differently from his usual self.

Frank clears his throat and looks at you in a strange way. He still hasn't said a word. *Poor fellow*, you think. *I wonder what's bothering him.* "Hey, Frank, you didn't call me in here for nothing," you say. "So what's it all about?"

Then all of a sudden, you get an icy feeling in the small of your back, and the hair on your neck starts prickling. It's the animal instinct for survival. Some sixth sense tells you that something is very wrong. There's an enemy on the prowl, and you may be the prey.

Frank finally puts down the paper. "Joe," he says, in a half-agonizing, half-supplicating voice.

"Yes, Frank?"

He takes a deep breath. "There's no other way I can say it. We're going to have to terminate you."

His words stun you, and you find it difficult to breathe. You try to lock eyes with Frank, but he won't meet your gaze. Instead he seems to be looking over or around you, so much so that you turn around to see if someone may be standing in the doorway. No one is.

You look back at Frank. It has become perfectly clear in those heart-stopping moments that Frank has nothing more to say unless he is cornered and forced to say more. Then comes your anger. Eight lousy years are riding on this. All the struggling, the late hours, the missed dinners, the times you couldn't be there when your kids needed you, the blood and sweat and loyalty you gave to this job. "What the hell do you mean you're going to have to terminate me? If this is some kind of a joke, Frank, come off it!"

If you do one single thing with that outburst, you jar the zombie look from Frank's face. "I'm sorry, Joe. I only wish it was a joke. I'm dead serious, and I hate to be the one to break this kind of news to you."

"But what about my project?" you say. "It was only last month you told me I'm in line for a raise and a promotion. How can all that change in one month? And what will the client say?"

Now, finally, he looks you straight in the eye. "The client knows, Joe. In fact, the people there were the ones who asked for a change."

"I don't believe you!" you say. "I've got to hear it with my own ears!"

Frank indicates the telephone. "Be my guest," he says, and something dies inside you.

You wave away the idea of phoning. "All right, Frank," you say. "You've told me I'm through. Now, will you tell me why?"

Again he looks away. The silence is unbearable. He shrugs. "Chemistry, I guess. I'm getting it about third-hand. You must've stepped on some pretty big toes over at the factory. The only thing I know is what they tell me."

You look at him, your former friend. It's all over his face: *Wish this poor guy would get out of here. He's making me nervous.*

"One more thing, Frank," you say. "What do I tell them when they ask me why I left?"

Now he relaxes and almost smiles. "Simple. You resign."

You shake your head. *No way! you think. Does he think I'm an idiot? Resign, and I won't be eligible for unemployment insurance. My chances of getting my va-*

cation pay and any possible severance pay will probably be diminished. (And, depending on the provisions of your company's pension and/or profit-sharing plans, it may be to your advantage if you are fired instead of resigning.) "Not a chance!" you tell him and walk out.

Or maybe it happens differently. You've been feeling for some time that your boss really doesn't like working with women. Oh, you're not absolutely sure, but it seems rather obvious.

He's overly courtly in his dealings with you, much more so than with your men colleagues. You've noticed a definite selectivity when he passes out the assignments. "John, this looks like one you could handle. Meantime, Jane, why don't you check on the market for women between nineteen and forty-nine?"

So you do your work, with good grace. But because you can envision getting labeled the token female, you finally go in to see the boss. You ask him if you can take a crack at an assignment that isn't specifically woman-oriented. You sense a flicker of annoyance followed by excessive heartiness. Whereupon he lays on you the one project everyone in the company has been ducking, because it's a no-win situation. Since you're not much different from the others, you don't win either. And you give him the chance to do what he's been wanting to do all along—fire you. He replaces you with someone he feels more comfortable with—a man.

The most frustrating thing is that he did it all legally. If you hollered foul, you wouldn't be able to prove a thing. In fact, he'd probably label you a troublemaker, and there's no point in jeopardizing any chance of a nice reference. So you grit your teeth and vow not to get into a situation like this again if you can help it.

Here's another scenario. You come into the company at a high level—third person in the department. You fit in right from the beginning. Everyone likes your work, and, with a couple of exceptions, you get along well with the people. More than once your boss says, "Joe, I'm sure glad we hired you." It feels good. You feel secure. You like your work, the pay is good, and there are plenty of fringe benefits. You're set.

Then your boss calls you in one day and tells you, "Joe, I'm leaving."

You're dumbfounded. "You leaving? But you're in line for president! What kind of a deal did you get to throw away all this?"

He looks at you with a funny smile. "I don't have a deal."

It takes a few moments for this to sink in. You just sit there and look at him. Finally, you sort out your thoughts. "Are you telling me that someone around here fired you?"

"That's what happened," he says. "Les gave me the word yesterday."

You shake your head. "But you've been making that guy look good ever since I joined the company! Doesn't he realize that?"

Now he grins, and for the first time today, he looks like his old self. "And how he does! That's what's been bugging him all these years."

So you buy him a drink after work, and a few days later he's gone.

There's plenty of speculation about his successor. A couple of your colleagues prod you. "Joe, they've got a headhunter on this. Lord knows who we'll get over us. Why don't you ask Les for the job?"

"Me?" you say, not quite used to the idea.

"Sure, why not? You can handle it. You're good, and everyone likes you."

You think it over. It doesn't seem right to have to

ask for the job. Your work is highly visible. So if Les wants you for the spot, he knows where your office is.

You discuss it with your wife, who suggests that you ask for the job as self-protection. "Suppose they hire someone over you who turns out to hate your guts? You're very good, and you may seem like a threat. Or maybe the new boss will be a whiz kid and won't trust anyone over forty. Maybe even thirty. Then where would you be?"

But in all your years of working, you've never run into much of the deviousness and backstabbing that happens in many business situations, and your pride won't let you go in and ask Les for the job. You know you can handle it, but you simply sit and hope for the best. You watch the stream of applicants with attaché cases pass your office on the way to see Les, and you try to read their faces. Some look like your kind of person, and you find yourself hoping one of them will get it. Others look as if they'd be terrors to work for, and you wonder what will happen if Les chooses one of them.

Naturally, that's the kind Les picks. And you're one of the first to know. "Joe, I want you to meet Stan. Stan, Joe here is one of our solid workers. He'll be a big help to you, especially while you're getting settled in."

You put out your hand and say something because you're expected to. "Nice to meet you."

He nods. "Les tells me you've been doing a lot of pinch-hitting the last few weeks."

"You might call it that," you say. "Things came up, so we all pitched in."

He forgets to smile. You see naked hostility maybe mixed with a little fear. "I want to get with you real soon," he says, "so we can sort out what's what and see where you can be of the most value."

You nod. "Sure. Just say the word."

"I'll let you know."

It comes to you fast—your wife was right. You should have made a pitch for the job, because this guy is out to get you, and he doesn't even know you.

Things go downhill fast. You know you should start job hunting. But you're a valuable person around here. Why should anyone want to replace you and start from scratch? Besides, looking for work is no fun. So you let Stan tear away every shred of your self-respect, week after week, month after month. After a while, you begin to doubt yourself.

Then comes the double-cross. Stan passes along verbal instructions, which you carry out. Someone complains about the job, and Stan conveniently forgets you've done it just the way he asked for it.

The work dries up, and you're not invited to the three-day seminar in the mountains for the first time in all the years you've been with the company.

Then comes the day Stan drops into your office, an honor you haven't had very often. The soft, devious smile and then right to it: "Joe, I'm going to have to let you go."

It's not necessary to ask why. There's no appeal to Les, because Stan has been given a free hand. "Take all the time you need," he says. "We'll keep you on the payroll as long as we can."

It could have happened any one of a number of ways. The reason may not be as ego-deflating as being sought out and fired, but your situation is every bit as serious. Maybe there's been a merger, and suddenly there aren't enough corner offices to a floor. Maybe the boss's son or daughter just got out of business school and is starting near the top in the job you fought your way up to. Don't laugh. It happens often enough. Or maybe a new president wants to bring in his or her own staff.

There are almost as many reasons for getting fired as there are jobless people. And don't try to kid yourself.

You were fired. The sooner you can accept that fact and admit it to yourself and to others, the sooner you'll pick yourself up and get moving again.

I went through the ordeal three times within nine years. I tried employment agencies and headhunters (executive search firms), wrote letters, answered and placed ads, made cold calls, phoned friends, and collected unemployment insurance until it ran out. I lowered my sights and tried to convince myself that I didn't need much salary to get by. And I found out that the more I demeaned myself, the less people thought of me. They sensed my failure.

Finally I told myself, "No more!" I stopped my frantic pace and took stock. I reviewed what I had accomplished over the years and decided that I was a valuable person and that any company would be very lucky to gain my services.

That was the turning point. I devised a plan of action and followed it until I got a new job—a better job than the one I'd been thrown out of. And during the course of my efforts, I turned down a few other offers. This book is written to help you do the same.

2

Make the Best Deal Possible

Back to reality regarding your boss, Frank. You told him you wouldn't resign. You go back to your office and cool off, or perhaps you take off early and hit a bar or two. Maybe you go straight home.

Telling your wife or husband the bad news is a topic of its own, and we'll cover it in chapter four. But it's important not to shield anyone from the news. This can be an opportunity for you and your spouse to grow closer together, or, if you handle it poorly, to drift apart. Nothing else will matter as much as whether or not you tell the truth and how soon you tell it. It's almost impossible to keep anything this earth-shattering from someone you love and have shared your life with. So do it right away. If you have children, when and if you should tell them depends on a number of factors, including their age and maturity.

My advice is to leave the office immediately, go straight home, tell your spouse, and then sit down with him or her and talk over the entire situation. Getting out of the office will enable you to avoid any additional confrontations and forestall any bitter feelings that could work against you in your coming bargaining sessions.

Tomorrow things are bound to look better, and your initial shock will have worn off. There will be aftershocks again and again, much as in an earthquake. But chances are that, for a while, you'll experience a form of euphoria. That very important report due this week suddenly is no longer a problem. You couldn't care less. (Except that you know the report is very good, and you wonder who will take credit for it.) Another thing, that person who doesn't like you and has been trying to cut your throat— that's no longer a threat. There's something to be said for small blessings such as these, even in the midst of a disaster.

You take your time dressing and eating breakfast, then leave for the office fashionably late. When you arrive, nothing seems to have changed, except that the receptionist does seem a bit too friendly as you nod good morning. Word has undoubtedly gotten around, and everyone has something nice to say about the "deceased." If that term seems harsh, so be it. Because as far as most of the people around XYZ Company are concerned, you're dead! Perhaps a few of your friends (and you'll find out soon enough who they are) will have the decency and good taste to express their regrets in a straightforward manner, to offer help, and to avoid phony sunshine and platitudes.

You enter your office and note with satisfaction that you still have a desk. Your secretary has even filled your water carafe for you. You're touched.

Undoubtedly you'll be having another session with your boss today. This time, the velvet gloves will be off. The damage already has been done, and he or she is not going to be feeling nearly as guilty as yesterday. So it behooves you to be businesslike and to present your requests as forcefully and unemotionally as you can. Make up a list of things to discuss with your soon-to-be former boss.

It's possible that you may have a couple of things things working for you—you've done a good job, and your boss might have enough guilt feelings to make some concessions if you're smart enough to ask for them.

There are countless sets of circumstances surrounding getting fired. Your particular plan of action will have to be formulated to fit your situation.

Your boss, unlike Frank, might have been the bad guy in the scenario. If he or she has been out to get you, like Stan in chapter one, you probably won't feel comfortable negotiating with such a person.

Perhaps you've been caught in the mass firing of an entire department. It could happen if, for example, a particular product has been eliminated from a company's line. Mergers are bad news for many employees. The bottom line in most mergers is economizing. The first economy is usually the elimination of duplicate staffs.

Herbert Moss, president of Herbert Moss Associates of Los Angeles, a prestigious executive search firm, describes several situations. According to Mr. Moss, a new boss is one of the most prevalent causes of firings. Either the new boss wants his or her own team in and immediately cleans house, or you two don't get along, and he or she has the clout to chop you off. A division of a large corporation may be divested, as when the Justice Department forced Procter & Gamble to divest itself of Clorox. This naturally generates a lot of changes. Mr. Moss also mentioned the possibility of an economic crisis in a firm, at which time jobs are doubled up. In this case, the junior person usually goes.

If, in any of these cases, you find that you're not able to communicate with the person responsible for your dismissal, you have a couple of choices. You can ask around and determine who else in the company has the power to negotiate with you on your rights and options. Or you can protect your rights by engaging an attorney. The latter would probably be your last resort, considering the cost of legal help these days.

There's always the possibility that your company believes a dismissed employee should clean out his or her desk and leave the premises the same day. If so, and you aren't prepared to negotiate on such short notice, then make arrangements to come in and see the person designated to handle severance matters.

HOW TO DEAL WITH YOUR BOSS

To reiterate, there can be no one universal plan of action that would apply to all of the possible reasons for getting fired. But based on my own experience and on that of many others with whom I have spoken, you may want to follow these steps:

Establish That You Were Fired. This is of vital importance. Some companies do not give vacation pay to any employee who leaves voluntarily. Most would never give severance pay to anyone who resigns. And it's more difficult to establish your eligibility for unemployment insurance if you leave a job under your own power.

So make it perfectly clear that you understand you've been fired, and that although you don't like it, you're prepared to accept the situation, with all the perquisites that go with it. Forget those euphemisms of "seeking new areas of opportunity" or "surveying the field" or "pursuing personal interests." It's no longer necessary to be phony about it, if it ever was.

Year after year, as good people are chopped off in many industries (such as publishing, advertising, aerospace, and electronics in the 1960s; securities in the early 1970s; and teaching in the late 1970s), getting fired has at last lost its stigma. Many a good man or woman has fallen victim to a merger, too.

It's no disgrace to be fired. The exception is the person who has been discharged for dishonesty, incompetence, unacceptable behavior, or blatant laziness. But, hopefully, none of the above describes you. Don't pussyfoot around. You've been fired, and it hurts. But if you're man or woman enough to accept it and to admit it, you'll be pleasantly surprised at the amount of respect you'll get. The fact is that it has happened to a lot of very successful people at one time in their careers, which makes for a good deal of empathy toward you.

Insist on Your Vacation Pay. You're entitled to any vacation time you have coming, in the form of additional salary. Many reputable firms have that condition written into their employee handbooks, so there's seldom an occasion when an argument is necessary.

Ask for Severance Pay. It can't hurt to ask, can it? This kind of pay is more of a custom than an inalienable right. Some companies have never paid it. However, a valued employee may be able to shame a company into some kind of concession—perhaps even one week's severance pay for every year of service. One way to handle this is to use an assumptive approach. "Frank," you may say, "how much severance pay do I have coming?" If he hesitates, you may add, "I figure I have at least sixteen weeks for the eight years I've put out for you." You've asked for two weeks per year. You'd probably be willing to settle for one. In fact, anything you get will be gravy. And Frank may even think he has struck a good bargain.

Protect Your Vested Rights in a Profit-Sharing and/ or Pension Plan. Here's where you may receive an unexpected dividend as a result of being fired. It all depends on the individual plan your company has and the vesting formula of the plan.

There probably aren't two profit-sharing or pension plans that are exactly alike. They are all under federal regulation now, Public Law 93-406—the Employee Retirement Income Security Act of 1974, more commonly known as ERISA. You can ask your U.S. senator or representative to send you a copy. But be forewarned that it's 208 pages long and rather difficult to wade through. The material covers protection of employee-benefit rights, including ten sections on participation and vesting.

According to the Commissioner of Corporations Office in California, you are entitled only to whatever benefits are set forth in the articles of the pension plan you're in. Certain protections are offered across the board. However, there are many different vesting methods. Some accumulate a certain vesting percentage each year —for example, ten percent a year. It could be five percent or as much as twenty percent. The percentage depends on how your company's plan was set up.

Other plans have "cliff vesting," which means a participant has no vesting at all for a specified number of years, then all at once a large percentage or even the total amount is credited to his or her account. Some plans have vesting that is determined by a combination of age and years of service. And there are several methods of payment, ranging from immediate payout on separation from service to lump sum upon reaching retirement age.

If you have any questions or doubts, see a good tax accountant or lawyer. Be sure to bring along all of your records, annual accountings, and any other papers that will indicate how much is credited to your account.

Get a Commitment on References. You've worked hard and loyally for Frank for these eight years. Even saved his face on numerous occasions. There shouldn't be the slightest doubt but that he'll give you a good recommendation should anyone phone to ask about you. Right? Maybe. Once you're out the door, Frank may not feel a shred of loyalty toward you.

In fact, he may use this opportunity to take credit for some of your contributions through the years. To do this, he would have to downgrade you. So if you state on your resume that you were "responsible for instituting a new production system that saved the company three million dollars a year," and Frank would rather take credit for that himself, what do you think he's going to say if someone calls and asks him to confirm that fact from your resume?

Here's what you can do. Go over your resume with Frank at once or later, after you've revised it. (Chapter six is devoted to resumes. Read this chapter before completing yours.) Get him to agree that it's entirely accurate and that he will verify anything on it if called upon to do so. So much for that, at this point. Now all you have to worry about is whether or not he keeps his promise. We'll deal with that in chapter five.

If you were fired by a boss like Stan or by a boss you know does not think well of you, you may not feel comfortable asking for a reference. You may very well feel that this boss will give you a bad reference no matter how nicely you ask. We cover how to neutralize a bad reference in chapter nine.

Get an Extension on Medical and Hospital Insurance. If you're like most of us, you fear being naked, insurance-wise, if something dreadful happens to you or a member of your family. Major-medical coverage is the only protection most of us have from the financial setbacks brought on by catastrophes such as cancer, heart attack, and other medical problems that can run up the bills to astronomical amounts. Sadly, many group medical policies stop coverage the very day a person is terminated. Others provide for a one-month grace period. Check out this feature carefully. If your company's group policy cuts off coverage on termination day, you'll have to move fast.

If your husband or wife is working and has a group policy that can cover you, this is one worry you can forget. If this is not the case, you have a problem. So read on.

Oh, sure, there are ways for you to convert your group policy to individual coverage. But there's a large catch. You cannot retain the major-medical provision. And that's the part you really can't do without. Most of us can handle the smaller charges, even for a broken leg or a few days in the hospital. It's the long, drawn-out disasters that we can't handle. So ask for a few more days on the job, just enough time to take out a floater policy or some other coverage. We'll discuss interim insurance in chapter five.

Arrange for Office Space, a Telephone, and Secretarial Services. That is, get a commitment for them if you want them. You may rather get right out of there and never have to see the people who have summarily rejected you. In that case, skip over this section. But perhaps you'd rather play things close to the vest, pretend you're still working, and operate from a position of strength while job hunting. I personally do not subscribe to this method because it's a strain to make believe you're still working for XYZ Company. And more often than not, the person interviewing you doesn't really believe it. I would rather clear the air, level with my interviewer, and come off as an up-front individual who tells it like it is.

But if you'd rather work from the office, you deserve some cooperation from your ex-employer—namely a private office for a fixed period of time, the part-time services of a secretary, and a switchboard operator who doesn't give it all away when you get a phone call. You probably won't retain the office you've most recently occupied. That one will most likely be taken by your replacement. But the office they furnish to you should be reasonably comfortable, and you should have the services of your regular secretary on a limited basis. This much they owe you. If you want it, ask for it as though you have it coming to you, because you do.

It's a good idea to have a friend or your spouse phone you while you're occupying this temporary space. It will help you to find out what kind of an attitude the switchboard operator, the secretaries, and other office personnel have about your present status. This way, you'll be able to take steps to correct any deficiencies before they do some harm to your job-hunting efforts.

If the idea of this cloak-and-dagger stuff bothers you, think of it this way. You're engaged in a life-and-death struggle to salvage your career and to preserve your life-style. This is war, with no holds barred. Only the strong survive. So be strong and do whatever has to be done.

Ask Your Boss for Help. He or she may offer to furnish you with some job leads. If not, then ask for them. Give your boss the opportunity to be nice. "Look, you of all people know the kind of job I'm capable of doing," you may say. "Do you have any friends you can send me to?" or "Do you know of any job openings you think I could fill?" You may be surprised at the effort put out on your behalf.

BEFORE YOU LEAVE THE OFFICE

After you're finished discussing your requests with your boss, there are two other important steps you may wish to take before you leave the office's premises (assuming you are not going to use the office to look for a job).

Ask Anyone or Everyone for Help. Please don't be the invisible man or woman during your remaining days on the job. Visit every friend and acquaintance within the company—you'll have enough empathy working for you to take a bath in bathos! Get all the contacts you can. Ask your colleagues to make phone calls for you. Many will be helpful, because, deep down, they know that there but for the grace of God go they.

You may find that some will use your predicament as an opportunity to build up their own egos, to prove that they're very big in the business, with a wealth of friends "out there." Good. Let them have all the credit in the world for furnishing you with some real live leads.

Get going on all this the first day or as soon as possible. Try to cover them all the first week for sure. The time will come all too soon when your colleagues' sympathy for you will wear thin. Then, immersed in their own problems, they'll figuratively cross the street to avoid running into you. So before sympathy changes to discomfort, get in your bid for all the good will, phone calls, and friendly leads you can get.

If you're lucky, one of the contacts will pay off with a job offer. Don't count on it, but it could happen. Then you'd be able to skip over some of the following chapters. But you wouldn't mind doing that!

Follow the "Scorched Earth" Policy. You're moving out—lock, stock, and barrel. Or you're shifting to a smaller office with no windows—just bare walls, a desk, and a telephone. The last thing you should do before moving out of your regular office is to comb your files and remove all your undeveloped ideas. If they've been developed and submitted, they belong to the company. But what about the ones you've worked up on your own time, the ones you've been planning to ram through the next time? Some of them are good, workable ideas. Do you want to leave them for your successor to pick up and take credit for? Or do you want to take them with you, just in case they are applicable to a new problem on your next job? No tough decision here. Simply have the maintenance people bring up a couple of cardboard cartons, fill them with your personal files, and take the cartons home.

And now, if you've followed the points outlined, you're ready to move on to the next steps in your comeback.

3

Tell 'Em You Were Fired

From the day you clean out your desk and ride down in the elevator for the last time, you'll have one question thrown at you more than any other: "What happened?" How you answer it will have a great deal to do with your morale, your frame of mind, and the image you show the world.

You've just picked up that final paycheck, said your good-byes to the people you'll miss, and taken the elevator downstairs. You're in an expansive mood for some obscure reason, so you almost say good-bye to the elevator starter, a kindly, graying ex-cop who always has a friendly word for you. But something holds you back. You hold your tongue, probably because the explanations are getting more painful each time you're forced to give them.

Surely there can be no single, all-purpose explanation that would be satisfactory for all occasions. Generally, you can divide the people you come in contact with into two groups—those who care and those who don't.

GROUP ONE—THOSE WHO CARE

The first group should get the whole truth. In this group fall your family, your close relatives, and your real friends. Anything less than complete candor may be interpreted as meaning either that you don't trust them or that you don't have enough respect for them to be certain of their reaction to the news.

Also in group one should fall all the people who are, have been, or will be involved in your business life, in any capacity. Fellow employees, direct superiors or subordinates, secretaries, customers, suppliers, competitors, and so on. Also, most importantly, the people who will be interviewing you during your job-hunting period.

Why should you level with all these people? For one thing, as we'll discuss later in this chapter, honesty is the only policy when you're on a job interview. And for another, you have pride and self-respect. The business world has more than its share of phonies—people who never say what they mean or mean what they say. Certainly you don't want to be included in that group. These people, when fired for whatever reason, carry a sackful of clichés to fit the situation, such as "I'm taking a breather," "surveying the field," "exploring new avenues," "examining options," or "reappraising my goals." The truth is that no one believes these reasons.

But you're much too smart to handle it that way. And much too honest. Whether you've been working for two, five, fifteen, or twenty-five years, you've invested too much of yourself in your career to throw it all away by using such transparent self-deception. Joe or Jane Bailey is a name that elicits respect, even admiration. There will be no furtive smirking behind your back, because you're going to be completely honest.

GROUP TWO—THOSE WHO DON'T CARE

With these people, you must be more flexible. The rest of humanity falls into this catchall category. These are the people who are outside your orbit—casual acquaintances or total strangers. They include the elevator starter you almost said good-bye to and most of the tradespeople you deal with, both at home and elsewhere. The elevator starter probably would have been shocked to learn you'd been fired and would have reacted warmly. But you have to draw the line somewhere.

People in group two, given the knowledge that you're out of work and that you actually were fired, may mention it in casual conversation or gossip. The fact that they may not do it maliciously is of little consequence—they are doing it. Under certain circumstances, it could work against you. So you must decide on an individual basis how to handle it with these people.

Here's an example: You're being considered for a top job by a certain firm. Unbeknownst to you, one of the company executives lives in your neighborhood. What if your postal carrier, happening to meet up with the gentleman at his front door and engaging him in idle conversation, should discover that this man worked in the same industry as you do? Isn't it possible that the postal carrier might drop some remarks such as, "Ms. Bailey down the street works in the advertising business too. That is, she did until she was let go last month." Coming from you, the fact that you were fired stands out as an honest statement. Coming from your postal carrier, no matter how well-intentioned he or she is, it has the effect of a piece of gossip.

There can be situations where there is no clear-cut line between groups one and two. This is where your judgment will have to take over, along with a gut feeling. If a certain individual is truly interested in your welfare, you can't afford not to confide.

There's another advantage to the truth. You only have to say it once. What person in his or her right mind would say it if it wasn't true? Now whatever you say within reason has more of a chance of being taken at face value.

I asked two executives who make their livings interviewing high-salaried men and women how they felt about the way their prospects answered questions such as "What happened?" and "Why did you leave your last job?" Both are heads of executive search firms, who have to be extremely careful whom they present to their clients. Paul Norsell of Paul Norsell & Associates, Los Angeles, said, "You must be completely honest. If I am interviewing a candidate, I don't want to have any surprises later on. I simply cannot tolerate dishonesty of any nature, and that includes misinformation. The same thing goes for my clients."

Herb Moss, previously quoted in chapter two, said, "It's essential that you tell the truth. If you don't, you're going to be found out eventually. The best policy is to be honest and brief about it. Whatever happened to you has probably happened to dozens before you!"

So you should be prepared to be asked what happened. The question may be posed for a variety of reasons, depending on who is asking it. It may be a co-worker commiserating with you about your bad luck, saying,

"How could they do this to you? Why, you were carrying that whole department!" Someone who dislikes your ex-boss may have his or her own motive for finding something out. "What happened?" can be a loaded question, so handle it with care.

A prospective employer may be measuring your character by the manner in which you answer. If you put the knock on someone, even if he or she deserves it, it may demean you. Therefore, if while you're being interviewed, you can't say something positive about your last boss and/or company, keep your lips buttoned. Let the interviewer read between the lines. It's much more dignified.

As a rule of thumb, you rarely will make a mistake by giving the reason you were given. If you don't agree with it, say so. For instance, "They said I was overqualified for the job I was filling. But I can't agree with that assessment. I've presented half a dozen proposals that would have made my department more productive and justified my salary. I'd like to show you one of those ideas."

Do some judicious editing, especially if the whole truth is a long, drawn-out horror story, such as the situation with the new boss, Stan (described in chapter one), who was out to get you and finally did. No one wants to listen to this long a narrative, even though every word is true. It comes off sounding more like self-pity than anything else. In this type of situation, brevity is imperative. You may say, "There was a change in supervisors. My new boss and I simply didn't hit it off." An answer such as this makes you appear reasonable. The person interviewing you will probably be sensitive enough to read between the lines. He or she will probably respect you for your evenhanded attitude.

WAS IT REALLY AWFUL?

If the place you worked was intolerable, it may be wise to say so flat out. You'll be surprised how often it won't be a surprise. Word usually gets around about that kind of a company. And if there has been a steady stream of applicants around town, all from the same place, it lends credence to your statement.

Sometimes it's not what you say, but how you say it. You might hesitate before saying reluctantly, "I don't like to bad-mouth a company that has been paying me good money for X years. But there's no other way I can put it than this. XYZ Company just isn't a pleasant place to work. I gave it my best shot all the while I was there." You've been honest, but not vindictive. You've come off looking good.

WAS IT YOUR FAULT?

What if you were fired for doing a lousy job? You're going to have to look at yourself as objectively as is humanly possible. Ask yourself whether or not it might be your own fault that you were asked to leave. If you can't be objective, ask a co-worker friend for his or her opinion and insist on candor.

There might have been extenuating circumstances, such as poor communications or a misunderstanding. Or maybe you had a boss who doesn't know how to delegate responsibility but is all too willing to point the finger at someone if things go wrong.

Whatever the reason, try to accentuate the positive. You can say something like, "I enjoyed many facets of my work there, but I never could get a handle on the chain of command. It was difficult to find out what was expected of me until it was too late. I blame myself as much as I do anyone else." You sound reasonable, but it's obvious that you feel the major blame goes on XYZ Company. Not a perfect solution, but not unacceptable either. You can even add, "One thing I've learned is that I want to really know what's expected of me before I accept my next job." That shows a positive attitude. If you did a lousy job, and it was all your fault, then you have a problem. You won't get a satisfactory reference from your ex-employer. You'll have to ask yourself if you're suited for this particular occupation, whether you were lazy or obstinate, or what other reason there could be for your failure. Perhaps your ex-boss will tell you.

When you do discover the reason, you must take steps to correct your deficiencies. Perhaps you just were not ready for that much responsibility. If so, scale down your ambition and take a less demanding job. When you master that job, you'll be prepared to move up to more responsibility. If this is your case, you could tell the interviewer that you see now that you reached too high too fast. You're ambitious, and you want to do a good job. But now you realize that you need a strong base on which to build. Such candor could be refreshing to a fair-minded person. If he or she isn't favorably impressed with your attitude, some other interviewer will be.

"HOW COULD THEY DO THIS TO YOU?"

This is quite another question, usually delivered with a sympathetic inflection. Be very careful here. It contains a built-in invitation to wallow in self-pity or to criticize your ex-company. Resist the temptation. The less said, the better. One way to deflect such a question would be to say, "There wasn't anything personal involved—it was strictly a business decision." You probably will never get this sort of question from an interviewer. It's the insider in the company who's probably trying to draw you out who usually asks it. Sometimes a shrug will be sufficient.

DON'T FEEL DISGRACED

Back in the "old days," when a person was fired, he or she might as well have had a red X marked in the middle of his or her forehead. There was a definite stigma attached to being fired, something akin to being drummed out of the regiment and having your epaulets torn from your uniform.

But a lot of things have changed since those days. World War II came along, and with it a working population that was restless and mobile. People quit jobs. People tried jobs just to see if they might like the work. And they were let go if they couldn't cut the mustard.

Then came the various booms in petrochemicals, aerospace, electronics, microcircuits, and other high-technology pursuits. Huge government contracts were awarded, and many contracts were terminated as abruptly as they had been established. Getting fired started to lose the stigma it previously bore.

The advertising business has always been one where it's understood that good people constantly get fired. When a large account moves, there simply isn't enough income left to pay the people. Everyone in the business understands and accepts this fact of business life.

A typical example of this was the company I worked for from 1972 to 1977. Parker Advertising of Palos Verdes, California, was an advertising agency built around one account—Nissan Motor Corporation, the maker of the Datsun automobile. Parker had handled Datsun since its introduction into the United States around 1960. We did service other accounts, but well over eighty percent of the $35 million in billing was on Datsun.

Then, on March 30, 1977, Datsun informed Parker Advertising that they were withdrawing their business in ninety days. The result was that the agency closed its doors on June 30th, and more than a hundred excellent people were thrown onto the west coast job market.

Most of them soon found other jobs in the industry, many better than the ones they were forced out of. A wave of sympathy seemed to sweep over the entire advertising business. People went out of their way to help the out-of-work men and women who had been on the Datsun account. Here was a textbook case of not needing any explanation other than, "My agency has gone out of business with the loss of the Datsun account."

However, seldom do you have the advantage of a ready-made and completely believable reason for being thrown out of work. More commonly, when you've been singled out as someone an organization no longer needs or wants for whatever reason, you're suspect to a certain degree. How you handle this situation will have a lot to do with the reactions of other people toward you.

Whatever the circumstances, be neither hangdog nor overly aggressive about what happened. Either attitude could trigger an unfavorable response from many people. Hold your head high. Tell yourself that you've been a valuable asset for most of your business life and that you're ready to be one again. The company that hires you will be getting an outstanding employee. Tell yourself that it's no disgrace to lose one's job, that one company's mistake can be another company's good fortune. When you feel this way inside, it's bound to show!

4

Level With
Your Family

Whether you're married, living with someone, or single, you probably have people who should be let in on your problem. There will be different circumstances in every person's life. Your financial condition and the importance of the job to you (either this job in particular or having a job in general) are determining factors in how difficult it will be to break the news. In a single-parent household, the problem is how much to tell the children, which we'll talk about later in this chapter. It is of utmost importance to tell the people who should know—and promptly. Don't make the mistake of trying to predict their reactions, thus attempting to shield them from the unpleasant news. If you love, trust, and respect them, give them credit for being mature enough and tough enough to take the bad news. Share the hard times as well as the good ones.

The situation that appears to be the most difficult to handle is that of the person, usually the man, who is the sole support of the family. The older the man and the more children and financial commitments involved, the harder it will be to tell his wife; there's more on the line than the blow of being rejected. Maybe you've heard of cases where a husband has lost his job and tried to cover it up by ostensibly leaving for the office, day after day. Actually he killed time in the movies or at the library. In nice weather, he frequented park benches. This is not for you. Coping with the loss of a job is a rough assignment that can wreak havoc with your well-being. You need encouragement, cooperation, sacrifices, and unadulterated love.

So the very day they lower the boom on you is the day you should tell your spouse and/or your family. You've just gotten the word yourself, and you're angry, shocked, and shaken. You're on your way home by car, bus, train, or taxi, wracking your brain for the right words to use. Take my advice, and don't spend any time thinking up a story. There's no such thing as the ideal way to break this kind of bad news. The only sensible way is to get your spouse alone and quietly tell the plain, unvarnished truth.

I was forced to do this three different times. The first time was as awful for my wife as it was for me. Our attitude was simply, "This can't be happening to us!" In the past, the only time I had ever changed jobs was when I received a better offer. Upward mobility had been the watchword. Now in one quick, terrible moment, my job had irrevocably rejected me.

I drove home to find a house full of children, our three plus some of their friends. I had to keep the news bottled up inside me until just before dinner. Then my wife and I were finally alone in the kitchen. "Al let me go today," I told her, trying to sound calm.

She looked at me, puzzled. "Let you go where?"

I didn't want to use the word, but it was necessary. "He fired me."

It still didn't register. She shook her head. "You're joking, aren't you?"

"I wish I were," I said. Then it did get through to her. We held each other and cried. Later, after dinner, we took a walk in our neighborhood on the balmy October evening. We were calmer now and more prone to look at the bright side. After all, I'd never been out of work since I'd left college.

"I'll be able to start that novel now," I said. "Besides, I'll probably have a better job before my salary stops." That's how little I knew about the job-hunting market. Jobs like mine were very scarce, especially on the west coast. It was sixteen months before I was back on a payroll full time.

The second time I was fired was entirely different. The people I worked for were as hard as nails. I'd been out for two weeks with a devastating case of flu. The first day back, I was still weak. That's when the general manager sent word he wanted to see me. Since it was the first anniversary of my starting date, I honestly thought he was going to tell me I was getting a nice raise.

But he wasted no time lowering the boom. I wasn't creative enough, he told me. He wanted me to clean out my desk and leave that day. I refused and held out for a week. Somehow I couldn't bring myself to tell my wife that day. She was weakened from the same flu bug. So I bought a little time and bottled it up inside for a week.

Looking back, it was probably the worst thing I could have done. My wife sensed that something was wrong. But she never guessed what it was. How could she have? I'd been given added responsibility just two months before!

Then one week later, I loaded my car with all my files, drove home, and told her. This time we were both toughened veterans of the unemployment wars, so it didn't hurt as much. We knew all the right things to do by now. We decided that nothing or nobody could hurt us. And that's why I regretted withholding the truth for a full week.

The third time there was no doubt in my mind. I went straight home with the news. Four years of hard work and loyalty to my job had gone down the drain. My wife and I packed a couple of bags and took off for a long weekend in San Diego. We used the days to plan our strategy. It was a happy time for us, and we both felt we had never been closer.

I'm thoroughly convinced that if you love and trust your wife, you owe it to her to tell her right away. Give her the opportunity to share your burden for better or for worse. Isn't that what it's all about? There will be rough days ahead, times when you two may be at logger-heads. But you will always have the knowledge that you're a team, a partnership of trust and love.

Telling children, parents, brothers, sisters, and other relatives is different. It's best to handle each situation individually. With your children, it would depend principally on their ages and maturity. You'll have to use your judgment as to when you tell them, what you tell them, or if you should tell them at all.

Children under five are oblivious to the consequences of unemployment. All they know is that Daddy and/or Mommy goes to the office or factory and brings home money. With this age group, the less said, the better.

Boys and girls from six up to thirteen or fourteen are insecure and vulnerable. If the father is the sole or main support of the family, these children may equate their father's job loss with all kinds of impermanence, whether or not it is justified. They're wrapped up in their own lives, so, depending upon your occupation, it should be fairly easy for you to let them think you're leading a normal workaday life while you're actually job hunting. Sometimes the explanation that you are looking for a better job is enough to satisfy them. Deep down, they may not want to know any more than that.

Teenagers of fifteen and over are also wrapped up in their friends and activities. So unless they're exceptional, they may not spend much time worrying about your problem, unless it looks as though they might be affected personally. Situations that would make it difficult for them may make it the same for you, such as the slightest hint that your unemployment may lead to a job in another part of the country, far away from their pals, or the prospect that something that was half-promised—a car, a stereo, a guitar—may not be delivered. In the final analysis, times such as these are when you discover whether or not you've raised your teenagers properly.

So tell your youngsters early in the game. Take them into your confidence, telling them exactly what happened and what it could mean to the family. Explain that it may be a while before you can land a job as good as the one you've just left, and that you and mom will need lots of help and moral support. Tell them that you know you can count on them. If they're the right kind of kids, they'll probably respond positively, proud to be treated as adults. Then you'll all feel close as a real family should.

If, on the other hand, they sulk and feel put upon, you've probably already had problems with them. So this attitude will come as no surprise. The problems may magnify for a while. You'll have to play it an inning at a time.

Your parents pose an entirely different problem. They're probably from the generation that believed in staying with one job for a lifetime if possible. Perhaps they survived the Great Depression and have a magnified fear of unemployment. This was the situation with my widowed mother. Since she lived three thousand miles away, I decided not to tell her. I was certain that I'd have my new job long before her next visit to California. How wrong I was! When she came out several months later, I was doing some consulting work and free-lance writing, but I pretended it was for my old job. She was far too smart to be fooled for very long. "You don't have a job, do you?" she asked me one day. Then I realized that it was past time to tell her.

The bottom line is that you just have to feel your way. Brothers and sisters, most likely near your own age, probably should be told. They may have friends who could furnish you with leads. Uncles and aunts are individual cases, too. You never know who may know the chairman of the board of a very influential company. So you want to get the word out and let the chips fall as they may. Just as a pebble thrown into a pond sends ripples in widening circles, so every contact you make generates a lot more probabilities of fresh job leads.

5

Before
You Start
the Job Hunt

It would be a mistake for you to start out the very next day to look for a new job. You need some quiet time for reflection. You ought to evaluate what has happened to you and consider how it may affect your career goals. There are also some crucial practical matters to which you should turn your attention before pursuing your job hunt. Then you will feel free to go all out toward finding another job.

ARRANGE FOR INTERIM INSURANCE

Here's how I did it two different times. The first time, I called the insurance agent who handled my life, auto, and home insurance. He did some searching and was able to find a policy that had major-medical coverage as a by-product. The principal coverage increased my liability for injury to someone around my home to one million dollars. It was called a success policy, which proba-

1

bly meant that by the time one gets successful, it is necessary to guard that success against a disastrous damage suit. Then, as a rider, this policy had a major-medical clause with a $100,000 maximum benefit limit. The catch was that it had a $10,000 deductible, which meant that I would have to pay the first $10,000, and the insurance company would pay eighty percent of the balance up to $100,000. The policy was not exactly ideal, but it did limit my payments to something I could handle, even though it would probably decimate my savings. This policy cost me about $100 a year. Bear in mind, however, that it was a rider on existing policies I had and couldn't be purchased separately.

The last time I changed jobs, I ran into the same problem of medical coverage. My company's policy provided for immediate cancellation of my coverage the very day I went off the payroll. I had the good fortune to have an insurance agent who, even though he carried no policy that fit my needs, found a competing one that did. He tipped me off that Allstate Insurance Company (a Sears subsidiary) has a Short-Term Health Policy specially created to help bridge the gap in hospital insurance, at a low cost, when you're between jobs.

Many firms have a waiting period before a new employee is eligible for group hospital protection. The Allstate plan provides either a 60-day or a 120-day policy, which pays up to $80 per day for as long as 365 days while the person covered is in the hospital, and eighty percent of other hospital medical expenses up to $2000. You can choose to have less paid per day and to have a lower maximum. You can cover just yourself or you and your entire family. It is a real investment in peace of mind, even though the coverage barely makes a dent in the huge hospital charges of today if a major illness should occur. Even though I had a new job waiting for me, I still had a 30-day waiting period before I could join the new firm's health plan. So I was covered and then some. At this writing, the policy is available at all Allstate Insurance Company offices, including those located in Sears stores, although the rates have most likely gone up since I took out my policy.

There are a number of other insurance companies covering this kind of problem. Washington National Insurance Company has a Medigap Plan. They offer a 90-day or 180-day plan with a $25,000 maximum. There are $100 deductible and $500 deductible policies, both paying eighty percent of the first $5000 in hospital and other medical expenses and one hundred percent of all expenses thenceforth up to the $25,000 maximum. Travelers Insurance Company has the Compac Plan, with a 60-day or a 120-day policy, covering $100 daily hospital room charges and other hospital expenses up to 500 days. Nationwide Life Insurance Company has a Short-Term Hospital and Surgical Plan with a choice of 60-day or 120-day policies; the terms are quite similar to the other plans described. Your insurance agent can probably find a plan for your situation among those mentioned here or among other plans that may be instituted subsequent to this writing.

You also need to take care of life insurance. That group life-insurance policy with the face value that you probably had with your company will cost you a fortune in premiums if you buy it as an individual.

It'll cost you a lot more even for individual term insurance. But if you shop around, you should find something adequate to cover you for a year. Term insurance has no cash value. It's protection, pure and simple—just what you need. Nowadays, even mail-order firms, including J. C. Penney, offer it to their customers. So do the larger department stores. If you have a mortgage on your house, the lending institution may offer term insurance. Oil companies offer it to credit-card customers. Why do I suggest a year's worth? Because even if you land your job, there's often a six-month or longer waiting period before you'll be accepted on the group life-insurance plan.

PROTECT YOURSELF FROM TAXES

If you are fortunate enough to come out of all this with a good chunk of cash and/or stock, you'll want to do whatever you can to keep as much of it as you can.

ERISA provides special rules for the taxation of payouts from pension and profit-sharing plans. For tax purposes, the payment is divided into two portions. The portion attributable to your participation in the plan before 1974 is taxed as long-term capital gain, which means that only forty percent of the amount is taxable. The portion attributable to post-1973 years of participation is taxed as ordinary income, for which ten-year forward averaging may be elected. With ten-year averaging, your payout is taxed at a much lower tax rate than if it were treated as ordinary income. If you wish, the Tax Reform Act of 1976 allows you to treat the capital gains portion, as well, of your payout as ordinary income subject to the special ten-year averaging rules.

Use of either of these two special tax breaks can result in increased after-tax dollars to you. The rules are a bit complicated, so you'll want to consult an accountant or lawyer on which decision is better for you.

In addition to the two tax breaks mentioned above, ERISA also allows you to avoid all immediate taxation on your retirement plan payout by starting an IRA (individual retirement account). I had my chance in 1977 when my advertising company lost the Datsun account and closed its doors. All of us who had stayed to the bitter end were paid off one hundred percent on our stock plan, profit-sharing plan, and pension plan. The letter that accompanied my check stated that this money was to be treated as ordinary income on federal and state income-tax returns.

I got together with my accountant to find out how to limit the tax bite. At the time, with the ERISA law still in flux, the best advice for me was to open an IRA. Congress instituted the IRA so that people who work for companies without retirement programs can set up their own plans and obtain the same type of tax relief. I started a "roll-over" IRA because I was rolling over the money from another pension plan into the IRA. Since my company had contributed all of the money, I was able to roll over the entire amount. If you have been contributing along with your company, you aren't allowed to roll over your personal contribution. You can, however, roll over the interest on your contribution.

An assistant vice-president in the Trust Special Services division of a west coast bank (who asked that she remain anonymous because of the bank's policy forbidding attributed statements) advised me for this book that the ground rules for IRAs keep changing and that one should always consult with a well-qualified accountant or lawyer before acting. You need not roll over all of your distribution if you don't wish to. However, under the new rules, if you elect to roll over only a portion of it, the amount that isn't rolled over will be taxed as ordinary income in the year received. And it won't be eligible for special capital gains treatment or for ten-year income averaging.

If you roll over property other than money (such as stock), the property rolled over must be the same property that was received in the distribution.

According to this trust officer, you should weigh your options carefully. If you need cash now, a partial IRA rollover may best suit your needs. But there could be conditions that would make it advantageous to keep all of the cash now and elect tax savings on the special capital gains or ten-year income averaging methods. For example, when you roll over money into an IRA, you can't touch the money until you're fifty-nine and one-half years old, and you must start taking distributions from it by the time you've reached seventy and one-half years of age. So let's imagine that you're sixty-five when you must choose what to do with your payout. You will only be entitled to keep your money in the rollover IRA for five and one-half years, and then it will be taxed as ordinary income. In this case, it can be to your advantage to take the money now as a capital gain and elect the ten-year income-averaging system. If, on the other hand, you are forty-five, a rollover IRA will protect you against being taxed on your payout for twenty-five and one-half years, which is very worthwhile. And all the interest your money earns will also be exempt from income tax until you take the money out.

If you do elect an IRA rollover, you must take care of it within sixty days after receiving your distribution. And that is the extent of your contribution to this particular IRA; it automatically freezes until you reach age fifty-nine and one-half. If your next employer doesn't offer a retirement or profit-sharing program, and you wish to handle your own retirement plan, you'll have to start another IRA. Toward this new one, you could contribute up to either $1500 per year or fifteen percent of your gross annual income, whichever is less.

But by the time you read this book, the rules may well have changed again. So it's important for you to consult a good tax attorney, accountant, or banker and make your judgment based on the best current advice.

APPLY FOR UNEMPLOYMENT
INSURANCE BENEFITS

One of the first things you should do is to apply for unemployment benefits. Some people figure that since they'll probably find a new job right away, there's no point in going through all the red tape and bother of applying for benefits. Others have ingrained prejudices against it. "I won't wait in line just to be humiliated by some civil servant prying into my personal business!" is one attitude I've discovered in some people who have never used unemployment insurance. Or "I've never taken a dollar of charity in my whole life, and I'm not starting now!"

Let's get some facts straight. I've used my unemployment insurance on three different occasions, and never once has anyone even made an attempt to humiliate me. Most of the state employees assigned to this vital program appear to have a great deal of empathy for the people they serve.

As for the idea that you'd be accepting charity, nothing could be further from the truth. Each state's unemployment insurance pool is funded by contributions from all the employers in the state. You've been helping your company make money for as long as you've been working for them. Part of those gross earnings you've helped to generate has gone into this insurance fund for the very purpose of helping you through the rough times until you find another job.

In fact, one of the obligations you'll undertake during the process is to register with and undergo an interview by a counselor in the State Employment Service. He or she is familiar with and involved in your industry, and it's quite possible that a job is listed that is just right for you.

Naturally, the process of registering for unemployment insurance entails the filling out of forms. You'll be interviewed by a counselor who must ascertain that you were really fired and didn't leave of your own volition. If you quit your job, you'll be thoroughly questioned as to your reasons. You'll be asked for the name of your immediate supervisor, and your story will be checked thoroughly. According to a spokesperson (who asked to remain anonymous) from the State of California Employment Development Department, there are cases where a person may resign for important and compelling reasons and be eligible for unemployment benefits. It's always to your advantage to file and not to assume that you aren't eligible. Since all the states honor each other's decision, there is very little difference, if any, in eligibility requirements. Be sure to check out your state's regulations; the best way to do this is by making application for your benefits.

If you're found eligible, you'll be given a specific day and time to report to the unemployment office each week. At this time, you'll be asked to sign a sworn statement that you haven't earned any money the previous week and that you've actually looked for a job. If you have earned a small amount of money, you'll still get some, but not all, of your unemployment insurance.

In California the maximum weekly unemployment at this writing is $104. That's $416 for four weeks, which can buy a lot of rent or groceries. So how can you walk away from that kind of money, especially when you're entitled to it? The maximum amount varies from state to state, but whatever the case, it's not exactly chicken-feed.

CHECK UP ON YOUR REFERENCES

There is a way to insure that your boss will keep to his or her word. For example, ask a good friend to make a phone call to Frank. The friend should work for a company that you might normally be expected to apply to. Your friend's conversation should go something like this: "I have a resume from a Mr. Joseph Bailey who says he worked for you for eight years. He lists a new production system as one of his contributions. Can you verify this?"

If your friend is convincing, Frank will say exactly what he'll be telling everyone else about you. And your friend can either put your fears to rest or tell you the bad news.

What if it is bad news? What if Frank said that it isn't so, that you didn't do what you said you did? This, in effect, is claiming that your resume is a pack of lies. Do you have any recourse?

You bet you do! The first thing you should do is to go right in and confront Frank. Tell him that you've been turned down for a very good job. The reason for the turndown is that he didn't verify your resume, as he promised he would. Then suggest that Frank join you in the president's office, where the three of you can thrash out who did what and when. If this doesn't drain the blood out of his face, nothing will.

If Frank backtracks and admits that he "made a mistake," then you make it clear that the next mistake may be his last. Tell him you've already met with your attorney, who is dying to file suit against both Frank and the company. In case Frank's wondering, it won't cost you a cent. Your attorney is quite willing to take the case on a contingency basis. Why? Because your lawyer knows it's a sure win and will make enough in actual and punitive damages to put the two of you on Easy Street. "Now," you ask Frank, "exactly what are you going to tell the next person who calls to check out my references?" I doubt if you'll have any more problems with Frank.

What if your ex-boss gives you a generally bad reference, and it's unwarranted? As long as people are people, personalities will clash, and this can be a possibility. In chapter nine, we will discuss ways to neutralize a bad reference. Briefly, it consists of hitting the situation head-on. Admit to your interviewer that Mr. Jones will probably be hypercritical of you. Tell why. Then offer other references within the company, especially some who rank higher than Mr. Jones.

Then, finally, if your ex-boss continues with the bad-mouthing, and you've done all you can to get it to stop, Herb Moss suggests that you put the matter in the hands of an attorney. That is a last resort; usually it won't have to reach that point.

ORDER STATIONERY

It's vitally important to have attractive, dignified personal stationery. Your letterhead will be the first contact you'll have with many prospective employers. If you use blank paper and envelopes from the five-and-dime store, it will say something about your self-esteem. If you use business stationery from your former employer, with the old address crossed out, it will say something even louder. You want your letterhead to say "Here is a worthwhile person who can do an outstanding job for you."

What you need is a fine business stationery in 8½" by 11" sheets, with corresponding number 10 envelopes. Splurge on fine paper stock. Buy from a reliable printer and check out the full selection of typefaces. You want something that looks like you. If you see yourself as bold and decisive, you may want a bold but tasteful typeface. If you wish to project the laid-back, subtle personality, look for a typeface that gets across that feeling.

But don't allow the printer to palm off something on

you that doesn't feel right. You may do much better to find yourself a small design studio and pay the artist a fee to select the right typeface and set your name and address. The same typesetting will suffice for the letterhead, the envelope, and the business cards. It should not be extremely expensive and is well worth it to present yourself as a successful individual.

Here's the design I chose:

Jerry Cowle
ADVERTISING COPY•
CAMPAIGNS • COLLATERAL
1000 Glenhaven Drive
Pacific Palisades, CA 90272
Phone (213) 459-1639

It's big and bold, which was the effect I wanted. I still use it for free-lance assignments.

GET AN ANSWERING SERVICE
OR MACHINE

I learned the value of a telephone answering service the hard way. It was shortly after I was fired for the first time. I did everything wrong during that traumatic period. That included not getting good stationery, not signing up right away for unemployment insurance (thus losing several hundred sorely needed dollars), and not getting an answering service.

My search for job leads had been extremely difficult and unproductive. I had only been in Los Angeles for fifteen months, and most of my contacts were in Chicago, where I didn't want to work anymore. I hadn't yet learned that I should have alerted every person I knew in Chicago of my situation, on the theory that one never knows who my contacts in Chicago might have known in Los Angeles.

I want you to profit from the mistakes I made. I finally had one of those interviews that has you walking out the door a foot off the floor. I was so sure I had that job signed, sealed, and delivered. All I had to do was to go home and wait for the man who interviewed me to phone and tell me when to start work. Or so I thought.

So I went home and told my wife all about it. We celebrated with dinner out that evening, leaving strict instructions with our older son to phone us at the restaurant if I received that call while we were away. It wasn't that I really expected the call that soon, but one never knows.

The next few weeks were hell. I was reluctant to do any more job hunting, fearful that I might not be on hand when the important call came. If I did leave the house, it was only when I was sure that my wife would be able to stay home and cover the telephone.

It was the middle of the summer, and all three of our children were home—just the perfect time to make good on our promise to take them to Catalina Island on the Great White Steamer. But we were afraid to be away from home for a full day with no one there to answer the telephone.

Finally, we reluctantly took off for Catalina. But we didn't really enjoy the trip. I had this recurring vision of a telephone ringing in an empty house. And I could see my prospective employer at that very moment riffling through the resumes of the other top candidates, since he was unable to reach me. The truth was that he never did phone me. I found that out later when I tried to call him and eventually got him after the seventh call.

For a small fee per month, I could have enjoyed a twenty-four-hour answering service and spared us all that agony and uncertainty. The next time around, that's exactly what I did. It was one of the best moves I could have made. It even led to such a good free-lance business that I had second thoughts about ever taking another full-time job.

You'll find telephone answering services listed in the Yellow Pages. There's usually a few days' waiting period and an initial connection fee. With a personal answering service, your calls will be answered with either your phone number or, if you wish, with "Ms. Jane Bailey's residence." If you'd prefer the response, "The Joe Bailey Company," because you're doing some consulting work, it will cost considerably more. You'll have to decide whether you think it's worth the difference. I never thought that it was.

There are also a number of reliable telephone answering machines ranging in price from fifty to several hundred dollars, depending on how many features you want. Some machines will actually give you your messages if you call your own telephone from outside. Whatever your choice, you'll find that your money will be well spent.

ARRANGE FOR OUTSIDE OFFICE SPACE

You should keep yourself on a businesslike regimen with regular business hours. It's difficult to attempt to work out of a home office, although sometimes impractical not to. Perhaps you have a friend who can spare a small office and the use of a telephone, or maybe you can barter a small portion of your time for office space.

When you have an office, you're downtown where the action is, just minutes away from most of your interviews. It gives you a better image to be contacted at a business address and phone, rather than at home where your wife or child may answer, expecting a personal call. It's more difficult to keep regular hours at home. There's always a temptation to linger over morning coffee and the newspaper, raid the refrigerator, take a nap, fix a screen door, or just plain loaf around. When you're at your office, you'll be putting one hundred percent of your efforts against the most important objective of all—getting back onto a payroll.

Hopefully, you'll be able to type your own letters and specialized resumes or can get your mate to assist you. Otherwise, you may be able to persuade a friend who owes you a favor to pitch in and help. Secretarial services charge rather high rates, so you'll want to use one only as a last resort.

POSTPONE THAT VACATION

You may decide that now's the ideal time to take that long-postponed vacation. Don't! This is one lovely urge you really ought to put on the back burner. The main thrust should be to get yourself connected.

The vacation can come later, before you start your new job. One of the first things you can ask for when you make your deal is to take some time off before you start. Your new employer will probably be happy to grant you this wish. After all, you don't start getting paid until you start working. So do it this way. Don't waste the time that's very, very precious—the few weeks of lead time when your name is still fresh in the job market. Months later, if you're unlucky enough to still be out of work, you may discover with dismay that you're considered to be stale goods. Your resume will have made the rounds. Now is when you're glamour merchandise on the job market. Don't dissipate this vital lead time by going on a vacation now. In fact, you're less likely to enjoy yourself with unemployment hanging over your head. If you go after you land your new job, the entire vacation will be a celebration.

TAKE A PERSONAL INVENTORY

This is the time to take a candid personal inventory of your strengths and weaknesses. Ask yourself whether any of what has happened could have been your own fault. Deal with the entire situation as objectively and honestly as you can; deceiving yourself is the worst kind of deceit.

You should also decide what it is that you want to offer to prospective employers. This section of your inventory can be a very important morale builder, because it tends to be an antidote to many of the unhappy and unpleasant things that have recently taken place. Once you have started listing all the things you have to offer, I'll bet anything that you'll feel like looking in the mirror and telling yourself, "You know something? You're pretty good!"

Now, let's talk about that candid personal inventory of your strengths and weaknesses. Even if you were utterly and completely dropped, there had to be certain things you did that contributed toward the showdown. Or things you should have done, but didn't do, that would have made you much less vulnerable.

To begin, ask yourself some tough questions. Were you completely reliable? Could your boss give you an assignment with full confidence that the job would be done quickly and be done right? Or, conversely, was it necessary to continually remind you that he or she needed the material and to nag you to get going on it? Were you a self-starter? When you saw something that needed doing, did you simply go ahead and do it, or did you always wait for someone to tell you it needed doing?

When something important was involved, did you stay with it regardless of the time? Or were you a five-o'clock-scholar who would walk out no matter what the deadline was?

How was your attitude? Did you always attack your

assignments with enthusiasm? Or did you constantly drag your feet and look sullen and put upon?

Try putting yourself in your boss's shoes and seeing yourself as others saw you. Then ask yourself, If I were my boss, would I have put up with me? It may come as a shock to you that your answer may be, "No way!"

Next make a detailed list of your strengths and weaknesses. Perhaps you're great at detail, never leave any loose ends, and are cheerful. You're well liked, you're good at math, you have a talent for anticipating problems before they happen, and you're a self-starter. All of these qualities can make you a very valuable employee.

On the other hand, perhaps you're impatient with those who don't think as fast as you do. You may be great at planning new techniques but impatient at following through on the detail work. Perhaps you treat your subordinates wonderfully but are very short with your superiors. This may indicate that you have a deep-rooted resentment of authority. Or perhaps it's the other way around—you're nice to your superiors and rotten to your subordinates. This may tab you as a bit of a bully. All of these shortcomings can be corrected, if you will admit they exist and then do something about them.

The final part of this inventory should be a list of all the reasons you would be an asset to the type of company you are soliciting. Be sure to include all your triumphs; your solid accomplishments; your education, attitude, and aims; and your own assessment of your potential. This is not meant to fulfill the functions of a resume, although you can fashion a very effective resume from these materials. This is basically a morale sheet. The only time you go to the trouble of putting all your good qualities down on paper is usually when you're looking for a job. It can be impressive and make you feel as if you're a really good buy for any company—which you are!

6

About
Your
Resume

The resume is a necessary tool for every job hunter. So much has been written on how to write one that you could practically paper the Great Wall of China with directions. Much of the advice is hot air, much is pedantic, and much is contradictory. A lot of it may be okay for young people fresh out of school, but you've paid your dues. For you, the simpler the better.

The main idea is that you should use a resume for what it really is—a summary of your qualifications. It should be specific but not so specific that it narrows the parameters of what you can do and what jobs you can fill. You shouldn't expect a resume to do any more than keep you in the running and hopefully stimulate enough interest on the part of a potential employer to generate a face-to-face interview.

A resume is a lot of things, some good and some bad. It attempts to be a one- or two-page distillation of a person's life and accomplishments. And that's an impossible task. How can a typewritten page or two be expected to

do justice to that complex, wonderful human being that
is you? Obviously, it can't.

WHAT A RESUME CAN AND CAN'T DO

At best, a resume can whet someone's appetite and
make him or her want to look you over. The person responsible for hiring someone for a position probably has
in mind a loose set of specifications for the job. If your
resume seems to match up with those specs on experience, education, and other qualifications, then you have
become a highly desirable commodity. In this case, your
resume probably will earn you an interview. The rest will
be up to you.

At worst, a resume can disqualify you before you even
step into the batter's box. This may be because many
personnel managers tend to use the resume in a negative
manner. Personnel people rarely know exactly what an
executive is seeking in a new employee; all they know is
that they have received a job requisition and that they are
supposed to deliver up a few select candidates. This is
what they are paid to do, and this is what they're going to
do. If they happen to overlook a nugget of pure gold in
the process, that's too bad.

It isn't always the personnel manager's fault. Often
the executive who needs an assistant cannot communicate his or her specifications in an understandable manner. And sometimes he or she has a gut feeling that really
can't be verbalized. As Louis Armstrong is reputed to
have said when someone asked him to define jazz: "If I
gotta define it, you'll never know." Feelings such as these
are valid but often intangible.

The average personnel manager gets dozens, sometimes hundreds, of resumes in reply to an ad for a single
opening. It becomes drudgery to whittle down this list of

prospects to perhaps three or four that the executive may want to see. So the attitude often becomes, "Let's see if I can eliminate this one." "This one" just may be yours.

Possibly you are better qualified for the opening than any other candidate. But a resume simply cannot reflect your warm personality, your alert manner, your desire to learn and grow, and your zest for accomplishment. A resume can only categorize you, sometimes unfairly. It can help you to be eliminated, but it can never get you hired.

I recently had an interesting conversation with an electronics engineer who had just started on a new job after a six-month period of job hunting. "I answered every ad I could find that even remotely matched my qualifications," he told me. "I also sent out over a hundred resumes to places I thought could use my kind of expertise. It was frustrating how few replies I got. And even when I followed my letter with a phone call, no one seemed to know who I was. One time there was an opening I knew I was right for. I sent my letter and resume by special delivery. But I never heard from them. This one disturbed me more than any of the others. I honestly couldn't imagine that they got an application from anyone better qualified than I was. So I phoned the personnel manager and asked her if she had had a chance to read my resume. She was very nice, but the tip-off was what she said to me: 'I'm sitting here looking at a stack of three hundred. I couldn't begin to find yours. Would you mind sending me another one, and marking it to my personal attention?'

"Well, that did it. I went right out to my printer and had him run off some more resumes. But this time I picked a wild chartreuse paper and told him to print the lettering in black. Then I sent one to this woman. I called her three days later and had no more than told her my name when she said, 'Oh, sure! The green resume. I have it in front of me right now!' "

While this is just one person's solution to the problem of being lost in the crowd, it says something about the pros and cons of the resume.

WHEN AND WHEN NOT
TO USE A RESUME

First off, you're going to have to prepare a resume and have it ready at all times. But don't just use it automatically. If you have managed to get an interview without using your resume, keep it that way as long as you can. Carry it in your briefcase or in your portfolio. Do everything you can to express to your interviewer the real you—the person who has spent a lifetime becoming who and what you are. If you can do that, and if you are skilled in putting yourself across, then your resume can be a very satisfactory piece to leave behind. In fact, be sure to leave enough blank space in the margins so that your interviewer can write things such as "Looks good, Nancy," or "Have George see this person re our new product group."

HOW TO GET STARTED
ON YOUR RESUME

Now that we've agreed that you're going to need one sooner or later, you'd better make it sooner. The first thing you should do is to make an inventory of all your experience and qualifications. Write down every job you ever held, even part-time ones when you were in school. You never know what will turn out to be helpful. For example, as a boy scout, I was one of the few in my troop who bothered to learn some of the rope splices. One day I was visiting the sporting goods factory in our town, trying to buy a slightly damaged infielder's mitt for half price. The factory owner was my neighbor, and he took me for a tour through the plant. They were finishing some tackling dummies for shipment to schools and colleges. He told me he was having trouble getting the metal ring spliced to the dummy's head. "Nobody knows how to splice any more," he complained.

I told him I knew how, and he hired me on the spot. I got a dollar for every eye splice I made for him—big money in those days. I used that experience on my early resumes. You'd be surprised what a conversation piece it turned out to be and how many prospective employers had been boy scouts themselves. So wrack your memory and put down anything that may be significant. You may not have room for it in the final draft, but now's the time to get everything down on paper.

Do the same for education—high school, night school, correspondence school, service schools, and college. Do it for all the clubs you've belonged to, hobbies you've enjoyed, and sports you've participated in.

Make a list of your noteworthy accomplishments on the job. Did you come up with an idea that helped cut costs? Did you suggest a new product or a new procedure? Did you help land a new customer? Did you take on a difficult assignment and master it? Do this for every job you've held. When you have it all down on paper, it may surprise even you.

Next write a short paragraph that describes what you believe would be the best use of your talents and abilities if you had your choice of jobs.

Once you have assembled all the raw material for your resume, you may be tempted to let a professional writer mold your material into a "surefire job-getter." Don't do it. Your resume should reflect you. It should be highly personal, because you are unique. Most of the professionals tend to squeeze everyone into one category or another, which makes for a dull and superficial product. Is there any wonder that this kind of a resume elicits a big yawn and a toss into the round file?

As I write this, I have in front of me a large ad from the Sunday edition of the *Los Angeles Times* for a resume kit selling for thirty dollars. The ad guarantees that the kit will get you a better job within four months or your money back. Sounds fair, doesn't it? But what if it doesn't deliver? Will your money back compensate you for the four months wasted if it wasn't the right way to present you? To put it simply, there is no substitute for writing your own individual resume. You don't have to be a skilled writer. You just have to organize your thoughts, and the resume will fall into place.

HOW TO WRITE YOUR RESUME

First take the inventory sheets with your job and educational background and sit down with some blank paper. Now you must decide the type of resume you will prepare. There are three major categories.

The Chronological Resume. This resume takes you year by year and job by job through your work history, with short, descriptive sentences on your responsibilities and accomplishments. It is by far the most common format. Some older applicants tend to shy away from this format, as do people who change jobs very often. They feel it reveals facts they'd rather not bring out. And since they're not required to indicate their age, they bypass the chronological format and opt for the next one. As I'll point out, this is a mistake.

The Qualifications Resume. This resume breaks down your job experience by the types of work you've done—the jobs you've handled. It doesn't mention specific companies or dates. The applicants I've mentioned above, ones who want to hide some fact or other, are tempted to use this one. In a word, don't! Herb Moss said, "It simply doesn't work! My clients want to know as much about an applicant as possible. You can't keep your age or your job record a secret. And if you try, then they'll assume you're covering up. Another thing—age isn't as important as you'd think. Ability and good health are more important."

Paul Norsell said, "There are very few genuine restrictions when my clients are looking for a man or woman to fill a position. If an applicant uses a qualifications resume, he or she is simply calling attention to an area that the prospective employer may never have thought important. For example, it's like advertising that you're over fifty. I'd never advise using it."

The Expository Resume. This is simply a thumbnail sketch of you, written in narrative form. Keep it brief and fact-packed. Be fresh, never trite. Don't tell too much.

Whichever form you choose, there are a few things you should never put down. Avoid discussing your salary requirements, your willingness to travel, or whether or not you would relocate. These should all be saved for your interview. If the interviewer is interested enough to want to see you, there's time enough to get down to these details. If the interviewer is on the fence, something extraneous in your resume may turn him or her off. Besides, the job might be so attractive that you would be willing to bend on salary, travel, or relocation. But you won't know that until you have your interview.

One important feature of any resume should be your objective—the description of the job you seek, what you think you can handle. Without it no one will know whether you're qualified in your own mind for the spot you're after. But try not to be so detailed or specific that you disqualify yourself for a job you could handle and might like. Keep your job description as broad as you can, so that a lot of jobs might fit under its umbrella. Keep in mind that many personnel people have tunnel vision. They're not trained to be imaginative and thus will not be trying to figure out where you might fit in. An overly specific job description may simply be a good excuse to disqualify you.

The exception to this advice is when you already know the parameters of the job you seek—for example, if you are applying for a very specific job. In this case, your best course is to write a very specific description of the job you're after, matching it up with the available job. And you'll want to select highlights of your past history that make you look qualified for the job. This means a complete rewrite of the resume, but it will be time well spent.

Keep your resume short. Keep it to one typewritten page, if at all possible. (And it is possible.) Use simple language. Avoid overripe prose or tired phrases. Don't furnish any more facts than necessary. Leave off age, race, and religion. It's against federal and state laws for anyone to ask you for such information. If you are a member of a minority group, why not let your qualifications speak for you at first? Later on at the interview, you might find you're at an advantage if you have treated it as a detail that is not pertinent to your job performance.

Your resume should include

- Your name, address, and daytime and evening phone numbers
- Your objective
- Your job experience
- Other experience (such as organizing a meeting of a club or anything else that may show skills applicable to the job you seek)
- Education

- Affiliations (clubs, public service organizations, and charities)
- Hobbies, leisure-time activities, and special skills and accomplishments
- Personal data (marital status, children, and health)

Don't give references. Don't even write that references will be furnished on request. Leave it to your interviewer to ask you for them.

There are no hard-and-fast rules for writing your resume. Use a format that you're comfortable with. Don't have a large quantity printed up in advance, for two good reasons. First, you shouldn't broadcast your resume to the four winds. It is not a good idea to send them out to every possible prospect, whether there is an opening or not. Because when there finally is a job open, someone may say, "Oh, yes, we have yours on file now. We'll call you if we decide to pursue it with you." You want to be fresh merchandise at the right time.

The second reason to keep the quantity down is that you want to retain flexibility. Always be ready to revise and slant your experience and education to fit the job opening. I don't mean that you'll digress from the facts. But you'll want to highlight certain parts of your experience for one job and a completely different set of facts for another one.

In general, don't answer ads with a resume unless it is requested. As I've said earlier, that's the easiest way to get disqualified. Instead write a good letter that tempts them with a small taste of your qualifications. You'll stand out from the crowd. You can give your resume later, at a time when it's asked for and has a much greater value.

7

It's a Cold World Out There

In the book *Born Free,* the husband and wife who raised Elsa from a lion cub decide to let her go back to her own environment. But they fear that such a long period of domestication has robbed her of her self-reliance. Something disturbingly similar takes place when a person is ensconced in an all-too-comfortable job. If anything happens to tear that person away from such a shelter, he or she must relearn those qualities of self-reliance and aggressiveness that have been blunted.

When you're a member of the team, everything is provided for you. You regularly get your paycheck. If you should become ill, even if it's merely a case of sniffles, you simply phone in and stay home. And you still get paid.

If it should be necessary for you or a member of your family to be hospitalized, the cost is not that alarming because you know that your group insurance will pay much of the bill, perhaps all of it. You may even have a dental plan to cushion you against large expenses.

You never need worry about whether or not you can buy life insurance—whether you can pass an insurance company's physical examination or whether you can afford adequate coverage for your age bracket. You're covered for a large face value on your company's group policy. As long as you work there, your family is well protected. You probably have long-term disability insurance, too, either privately administered or state-regulated. So even if something happens to you that prevents you from working for an extended period, most of your income keeps coming in.

You may find it easy to save by using the company's credit union, with your contribution deducted automatically each payday. You may be a participant in a company stock plan, whereby you elect a payroll deduction and the firm contributes a matching sum. These are easy forced-savings plans that the outsider can never hope to match. Then there are Christmas bonuses, paid vacations, company parties and picnics, business entertaining, gifts, free coffee, subsidized parking, and other pleasant little extras that may go with the territory.

A large company, with headquarters amid wooded countryside in the Westchester County suburbs of New York City used to arrange to pick up their employees at the commuter railroad station. They furnished new buses, air-conditioned in the hot weather, so that the employees wouldn't have to put up with the inconvenience and discomfort of public transportation. One dyed-in-the-wool company man, watching less fortunate folks waiting in the snow for a city bus, was overheard saying, "It's really cold out there."

What he said had a larger, more ominous meaning. The longer one remains in the bosom of a beneficent corporation, the colder it seems to be "out there." Just as a person's blood can thin from years of living in a warm climate, so can it figuratively thin through basking in the warmth of a Ma Bell or any one of her many generous cousins.

Then suddenly it's all taken away. "Naked came I into the world, and naked must I go out." Through Don Quixote, Miguel Cervantes tells this undeniable truth. But there's one other time when you're naked—right after you've been fired. Another way to put it is that you've been evicted from a warm corporate womb. (Or, if you can look at the positive side—you've been reborn.)

But how are you ever going to match the kind of solicitude a large company may offer for the well-being of its employees? The company mentioned above offers a bundle of benefits that amounts to virtually cradle-to-grave security, as long as one performs a reasonably satisfactory job. Imagine the shock, almost the bereavement, that must occur when all of these goodies suddenly are taken away.

What every company man or woman really needs is a wilderness survival course to cushion the shock of separation from the corporation. Unfortunately, most of us have the same viewpoint as many young people thinking about death. We figure that it will never happen to "us," but just to "them." Until one shocking day "us" becomes "them." Usually, it's too late to cushion the shock. All you can do is to pick yourself up off the canvas and get back into the battle—which is really what this book is all about.

NOW IT'S ALL UP TO YOU

Perhaps your company offered a comparable package. If so, you've been yanked away from a lot of security and fringe benefits, and you're going to have to pick up the pieces. You'll soon learn to get along without most of the perks of your former job; you've already begun to provide some of them for yourself if you've followed chapter five. The privileges were very nice. But plenty of people never had them and never missed them.

After you have arranged for the essential services outlined in chapter five and have perfected your resume, you can devote all your energies to the business of looking for work. Don't make the mistake of thinking that you'll probably land your new job in a week or two, so you can neglect those matters.

I hope that you do find a job fast. But if you don't, not having arranged for insurance, unemployment compensation, a telephone answering service or machine, and so forth, or not having analyzed your situation can really handicap you. And if you're lucky enough to find a new job right away, I doubt that you'll mind having accomplished those things.

Think of your job hunt as a genuine full-time job, with minimum hours of from nine to five, Monday through Friday. And, as you sometimes do on a job, take work home so that you don't fall behind on all the things that need to be done.

8

How to Generate Job Prospects

Forge ahead with your job hunt! Here are ways to begin and avenues to take after you've done the obvious.

CONTACT YOUR BUSINESS FRIENDS

This is probably the most important piece of advice in this book. If you've been a part of an industry for a considerable length of time, you're bound to be a known quantity to a number of people. Not too many of them are potential employers. But each one of them has a list of acquaintances that's probably as extensive as your own list. So you'll be widening your circle by geometric progression. Let's say you know fifty people in the industry, and each of them knows fifty more. That's twenty-five hundred people. It's much like a chain letter, but a lot more likely to pay off.

Who are these people? They're your clients, your customers, and your suppliers—the people your firm buys from and sells to. For example, if you sell office machines, they're the people in every company that ever bought a machine from you—every purchasing agent, every office manager, and every executive with whom you've had personal contact.

If you're with a law firm, these people are all the clients you've ever defended, represented, or helped plus the members of every competitive firm you've done business with on an adversary basis.

If you're with an advertising agency, as I am, these people are all the ad managers you ever worked with; all the film production people; all the recording engineers; and all the magazine, newspaper, radio, and television representatives. They're all the friendly competitors at all the other advertising agencies. Perhaps they've been worrying about the great job you've been doing on an account that competes with one of their accounts. Now you're offering them a golden opportunity to stop that worrying. Even if they can't hire you, they may be able to recommend you to someone else. And the ripples keep widening.

Who else? The editors of the trade magazines and newspapers that serve your industry. These professionals may already know about you or about some of your noteworthy accomplishments. They're usually wired in to the goings-on and to the job market in their industry and attend most of the major meetings and conventions. Enlist the help of these people if at all possible.

Tax your memory to dredge up the names of those friendly sorts you met at the last awards dinner and at the annual convention. Some may not remember you. Some won't want to be bothered, once they discover that you're no longer in a position to do them any good. But all you need is one person who knows what it's like to be "pounding the pavement" and perhaps has had someone offer a helping hand in an hour of need. It's worth the effort to contact everyone—repeat, everyone—you know on the chance that you'll find this one person.

ENLIST YOUR PERSONAL FRIENDS

Again, don't let any false pride get in the way. There is no longer a stigma attached to being unemployed. Too many people are standing in the unemployment insurance lines for you to start worrying about your image.

TELL YOUR NEIGHBORS

At least, tell the ones you like that you're looking for a job. It's not necessary for you to go into much detail about why you're looking, however. Tell your fellow club and/or lodge members; minister, rabbi, or priest; barber or hairdresser; bartender; and tailor. Tell your insurance agent, lawyer, doctor, and accountant. But be selective. If you have even the slightest doubt or uneasy feeling about any of these acquaintances, then don't say a thing. There is a certain type of person who derives satisfaction from seeing someone squirm. You don't want to give such a person this opportunity.

Every one of those you do see fit to tell knows a brand new circle of people. These ripples will spread wider and wider. All these people do a lot of talking with others they deal with day after day—men and women just like you, each with a different circle of friends. And so the word spreads. For example, I know a man whose twelve-year-old child, playing at a friend's house, happened to mention to the boy's parents that his father was looking for a job as a commercial artist. Coincidentally, the father of his friend owned his own design studio and was looking for an artist. The artist gladly followed his son's suggestion and phoned the studio owner. The call resulted in an interview and a better job. But suppose the out-of-work artist had sworn his son to secrecy, not wanting the world to know that he had been fired? So you see, there really isn't any room for false pride when you're job hunting.

ANSWER HELP-WANTED ADS

But don't pin all of your hopes on them. Some companies advertise simply to build up a file of good future prospects even though they have no immediate openings. Often these companies receive hundreds of replies for one job offer because they know all the key words to make the ads appealing. If you do answer an ad that describes a job you think you'd like, try to be original and put a little of your own uniqueness into your reply. Don't be stodgy.

A friend of mine once answered an ad for a job as a television copywriter by emphasizing that he knew all types of people and what motivated them. He stated that he had held a wide variety of jobs, including working on a garbage scow on the Chicago River. His letter stood out from the other hundred or so answers. He got the job.

If at all possible, find out about the company whose ad you are answering. (This may not be easy, as ads often give only a box number to respond to and do not list the name of the company. These are known as "blind ads.") Back when I was working in Detroit, I yearned to work for an advertising agency in Chicago that had just started to exhibit its greatness—the Leo Burnett Company. They ran an ad in *Advertising Age*. I knew the kind of work they did and liked—strong, simple statements with great impact. So I decided to tailor my reply to their specifications. I sent them a two-sentence letter, along with the requested resume. "Dear Sir," I wrote. "My foot will fit your glass slipper. When can I try it on? Sincerely yours, Jerry Cowle." Two days later they telegraphed me and invited me to come to Chicago at their expense for an interview. I took a plane there and was hired on the spot.

This letter might have really bombed if sent to another company. But that's just my point: It was a rifle shot directed straight to a susceptible target. If Burnett had been a different type of a company, I would have sent them a different letter.

I'm careful which blind ads I answer. There are situations in which prestigious companies must keep their identities confidential. But as mentioned above, a lot of companies advertise this way when no job exists, just to build up their files. And other, not-so-prestigious companies may advertise this way for reasons of their own. You'll have to judge each ad individually; this goes for ads that are signed, too.

Read between the lines. Many times you'll see an ad that reads something like this. The translations are inside the parentheses.

YOUNG COPY TIGER (so hungry you'll work for cat-food prices)? Talented, ready to move up (knows where the "E" key is on the typewriter and works cheap)? Rapidly growing agency (we started with nothing, and we've doubled our billings) has a fine lineup of aggressive clients (we have a fight on our hands to get our money out of them every month). If it's a challenge you're after (come with us, and we challenge—even defy—you to get some good work through), tell us all about yourself in a letter (then maybe, just maybe, we'll identify ourselves to you—but don't count on it), enclosing three of your best pieces of work (if we like them, we'll change the names and use them for our purposes). We offer the going salary (that's why our people are always going) with unlimited ceiling (our floor, unhappily, is limited by the minimum wage regulations) if you have what it takes (a strong sense of masochism). You'll live within minutes of our centrally located offices (to make it easy for you to stumble home after working far into the night). You'll enjoy an outstanding package of fringe benefits (every other weekend off, full half-hour lunches, and an office Christmas party). And you'll work with dedicated pros (so ancient they should have been dedicated with the building's cornerstone) who are never satisfied (you can say that again)! Write Box 25 (because if we signed this ad, you'd know it was a pack of lies!).

This is a rather farfetched little example, but you can have a little fun guessing what some ads really mean. After a while, you can teach yourself to spot the serious ones and screen out the garbage.

RUN YOUR OWN AD

Give a good deal of thought to the environment you want your ad to appear in. It might be in a newspaper, a trade magazine, *The Wall Street Journal*, or in a less obvious place, such as a publication you know is read by some of your top prospects.

Once you've decided where to say it, then the problem is what to say. After you've listed the vital facts, try to give your ad some character. Look at it from your potential employer's point of view. What can you offer him or her that will be intriguing and of value? You could say,

"Sold $20 million worth of machine tools last year." Or
"I can show you how to increase machine shop production by twenty-five percent." Or "Aggressive loan officer
doubled dollar volume of loans in two years." Or "Could
you use the copywriter who dreamed up 'Datsun Saves'
on your car account?" Make an offer they can't refuse.

RUN YOUR OWN
DIRECT-MAIL CAMPAIGN

Write a lot of letters and send out a lot of resumes.
Nothing new about this, is there? Well, maybe there is.
Because I mean write to everyone you've ever known in
your business life, going way back to your first job. Even
if you mowed the lawn of a businessman when you were
in high school, write and tell him what you're up to now.
If he liked your mowing job, he might want to recommend you to someone on the basis of what he knows
about your character. You just never know where your
next job lead will come from. Write to ex-associates
you've worked with, for, or over. Write old customers,
clients, suppliers, fellow club members, and service bud-
dies—everyone you know.

Let me give you a prime example of this technique
paying off. A man I know had been advertising account
executive in Los Angeles for the Southern California
Chrysler-Plymouth Dealer Association. Then his advertising agency lost the account and had to let Fred go. He
bounced around for a while, but nothing crystallized.
Months went by, and Fred was still without a job. He was
getting very discouraged and had convinced himself that
he'd tried absolutely every approach possible. He told
me that there really wasn't another thing he could do.

Then he decided one day that he might as well write
to everyone he had ever known during his business

career. He didn't miss a single person. The only thing it cost him was a little time (of which he had more than enough to spare) and some postage.

Then one fine day, out of the blue, the phone rang. It was a call to Fred from the manager of the Los Angeles office of a large, prestigious national advertising agency; Fred had no idea where the man had gotten his name. The manager asked Fred out to dinner and hired him the next week as account supervisor on a large savings and loan association account.

Fred took me to lunch soon afterward and told me how it all came about. One of his many letters was to an auto dealer in Chicago, a man who had admired Fred's ability in the distant past in handling a dealer association in the Chicago area. The week after receiving Fred's letter, the dealer had business in New York. So he showed the letter to a friend who was the executive vice-president of that large advertising agency. Along with the letter, the dealer praised Fred highly.

The advertising man knew that his Los Angeles office was looking for a good man. So he phoned the L.A. manager and asked him to take a look at Fred. The man did and hired him. After three months on the job, Fred had made such a fine impression that they promoted him to a bigger job in their home office.

It all started simply because Fred had the imagination to guess that even if his car-dealer friend couldn't offer him a job, he might know someone else who could.

CHECK YOUR INDUSTRY DIRECTORY

Whether you're a locomotive salesman or an electronics engineer, a directory of one kind or another of companies in your industry is most likely available at a nearby public library. Ask the reference librarian to help you locate such a directory if you need help. Make up a list of likely prospects from this directory. Do not rely on your memory alone, because you cannot expect to remember all of the possible places you might find a suitable job. Some of the smaller companies in your field that you may never have heard of could in reality be better prospects. They're leaner, younger, and still growing. They might be better places to move ahead than in many overgrown, sluggish Fortune 500 companies. In the directory, you'll find the names of the top executives listed with their specific areas of responsibility, so you'll be able to address your letter to an actual person rather than to Vice-President, Sales, ABC Corporation.

But no letter can do the whole job. In fact, any letter that isn't followed up with a phone call asking for an interview isn't worth the paper it's typed on. If you were to see all the letters received by the average person in a position to hire people, you'd realize that, no matter how courteous the recipient is, he or she just cannot respond personally to this deluge of mail. It usually boils down to one of these two circumstances: One applicant wrote such an outstanding letter and resume that he or she was contacted and asked to come in for an interview. Or, all other things being equal, the person with enough interest to follow up a letter with a telephone call generally got the interview.

CONTACT HEADHUNTERS AND EMPLOYMENT AGENCIES

No chapter concerned with generating job prospects could be complete without mentioning these important sources. However, since there is much material to cover on them, as well as on career preparation and guidance firms (a more recent development), an entire chapter, chapter ten, is devoted to this subject.

APPLY TO FORTY PLUS, INC.

If you're over forty, consider joining Forty Plus. It's a well-regarded self-help organization that has a very high rate of success in placing its members. There are Forty Plus offices in most large cities; their listings are in the telephone directory. Contact them for information about application.

Forty Plus members pay a modest initial tuition fee and a small monthly contribution to maintain their facilities. Each member contributes two days of work each week. But it's well worth it, because the Forty Plus approach has helped thousands of people to re-ignite their careers.

Once you're accepted for membership (and it isn't automatic by any means), you'll be helped in a multifaceted way to market yourself, all the way from your resume to the face-to-face interview. You'll be nudged into acquiring the proper attitude on what you have to offer an employer. In fact, you'll be forced to examine your qualifications for positions you might never have felt qualified to fill. It's a total packaging plan, and it has worked very well. After you find a job through the help of Forty Plus, you're obligated to be available as a loyal alumnus to help others in the same predicament that you were in.

CONTACT YOUR COLLEGE
ALUMNI ASSOCIATION

Your university or college's alumni association can be another source of job leads. Many top executives in large companies tend to favor alumni from their alma maters, all other factors being equal. That being so, they often contact the Alumni Placement Office and list their openings. It can't hurt to drop a line to your own college's placement office, listing your qualifications and enclosing a resume. Don't simply assume that their services are limited to recent graduates, because they really aren't.

STAY IN YOUR
INDUSTRY'S MAINSTREAM

This is one of the most important things you must do during this difficult period between jobs. Do it at all costs, because there may be a tendency on your part to pull in your horns and lick your wounds in privacy. Do not succumb. It's not a crime to have been fired. You're not a social outcast unless you allow yourself to feel like one.

Keep current with the journals in your industry. Push yourself to phone friends for lunch and to look up the dates of meetings of the business clubs and trade associations which you either belong to or may attend the meetings of as a guest because you work in that particular field. If there's an important convention coming up, attend if at all possible. It's a legitimate tax deduction, so that should soften the financial shock. And you'll be keeping your name and face in front of your choicest prospects.

If you're like a lot of people, and especially if you're not by nature the outgoing type, you may experience a certain amount of reluctance about picking up the telephone to call people and ask them for help. I had a real block about that. I just could not bring myself to phone even good friends. I was embarrassed to have to say, "What I really called you about was. . . ." It was a ridiculous attitude. When the roles had been reversed. I had always been happy to hear from old friends or acquaintances, even though I knew they might want me to do something for them. But when you're desperate, sometimes you don't think too clearly.

One day I confided my fear to a friend who had been

out of work for a long spell the year before. "Yes," he admitted, "I had the same problem. But I cured myself."

I asked him how. "You have to do it mechanically," he said. "Without thinking. I know this sounds crazy, but you simply pick up the phone, and with the other hand, you start dialing. It's that simple. You have to train your hands to do it for you."

I tried it, and it worked! Once that phone started ringing, I was past the barrier and so loosened up.

The main thing is not to drop out when you're trying to generate job openings. Keep abreast of your industry. Be aware of the important meetings and conventions. Those places are where more employment deals are consummated than almost anywhere else. And if you're there, looking prosperous and relaxed, you're going to get your share of leads.

9

Interviewing

It's an art to make the job interview come off perfectly, but that's your aim. The interview is the two-minute warning, the ninth inning, double overtime. It's where the buck stops and the rubber meets the road. Or as the baseball announcers are prone to say during the seventh game of the World Series, "There's no tomorrow."

This is not meant to give you a tense, do-or-die attitude as you approach an important interview but rather to impress upon you how necessary it is to prepare yourself thoroughly.

AVOID TELEPHONE INTERVIEWS

If the occasion arises when you are on the phone with a harassed personnel manager and he or she attempts to interview you then and there, back away. Use any excuse you can dream up. You may say, "I'm really not prepared to discuss my qualifications until I know more about the opening. May I have an appointment to see you in person?" Or "I don't think I can present myself properly unless I have the opportunity for a personal interview. Could we get together at our mutual convenience?" You get the idea. A telephone interview is a tool that personnel managers use to eliminate prospects rather than to qualify them.

If the opening is out of town, a telephone interview may be more convenient, but the disadvantages of a phone call are the same whether the opening is a mile away or across the continent. In these days of jet travel and relatively low fares, it's possible to be almost anywhere for an appointment with a day's notice.

Herb Moss is very emphatic about the disadvantages of a telephone interview for an out-of-town opening. "It simply isn't effective," he said. "You need face-to-face communication for something this important. If the company is genuinely interested in discussing the opportunity with you, they'll be more than happy to pay your travel expenses. Usually it's understood that they'll pick up the tab. But if you're at all in doubt, just ask."

LEARN ALL YOU CAN
ABOUT THE COMPANY

When you apply for a job, it's assumed by the interviewer that you know something about the company. After all, you could be spending years of your life there. Yet you'd be surprised how many applicants don't make the effort to find out what they can about the place where they aspire to spend a share of their working lives. It sounds basic, doesn't it? But many just don't bother.

You're different. You want to create the impression that you know and approve of the company you're trying to join. Do your best to surprise your interviewer with your knowledge of the company. Ask questions to fill in the gaps in your information. It's a good way to handle your interview, because you'll be getting your interviewer to do a good share of the talking. This way you can come off as a good listener.

Here are some of the facts you should find out about the company you'd like to join:

- What is its business? What does it manufacture or what service does it provide?
- Who are its prospective customers?
- Where does it carry on its business?
- Does it have branches, subsidiaries, and/or divisions?
- What kind of advertising does it use?
- How does it distribute its products and/or services —sales force, brokers, wholesalers, mail order, or a combination?
- Who are its competitors, and where does the company stand in relation to them?
- What is its growth pattern?
- Is the company's stock considered to be a good buy for investors?

Where do you find this type of information? If you're researching a publicly held company, it's all available. Look in Standard & Poor's reports and in Moody's investment guides, both available at any stockbroker's office. Go to your library and look up the company in the *Reader's Guide to Periodical Literature.* You'll find out what's been written about the company in business magazines such as *Fortune, Forbes,* and *Business Week* or if the company has been the subject of an article in a consumer magazine. Ask a stockbroker whose judgment you respect. Read the trade magazines. If you have a friend who works for another company in the same industry, ask him or her. Call the business editor of your daily newspaper. Ask the reference librarian for help in locating any other directories for your profession or industry.

LEARN ABOUT YOUR INTERVIEWER

You're way ahead of the game if you've been able to arrange an interview with the person who has the power to hire you, rather than with the personnel department. The next thing to do is to see if you can find out some facts about him or her. Look up the executive in *Who's Who in America* or in a more specific book for his or her industry. Ask your friends for information.

What is it that you're trying to discover? Anything that might be of help in setting a good tone for your talk. Perhaps he or she is a rabid football fan, a backpacker, or a jazz buff. You may never have an opening to use the information. But if you happen to see some object on his or her desk that relates to an interest you know about, the information may open the way for a pleasant turn in the conversation.

It pays to know ahead of time if your interviewer is a stickler for promptness and neatness or an arch-conservative or ultra-liberal. You don't want to try to curry favor by agreeing with whatever he or she says, but knowing when to be noncommittal is a big plus at this stage. You need all the help you can get when you're being interviewed, so do anything and everything you can to cut the odds.

Your interviewer may be a member of Alcoholics Anonymous or have a great dislike of tobacco. Sometimes questions that reflect set attitudes get inserted into the interview. If you have some advance information, you can cope with these curve balls better. For example, if you are aware that your interviewer is in the throes of a marital crisis, you won't be as likely to take personally a certain gruffness or sharpness on his or her part. No one is perfect, and it's often difficult for a person to leave all of his or her personal problems at home.

GET A STRONG START

Henry David Thoreau wrote, "Beware of all enterprises that require new clothes." With all due respect to the great philosopher and naturalist, there are times when we must face reality. First impressions are extremely important when you are being interviewed for a job. You need all the positive factors that you can muster working for you. One of them is to be well dressed and well groomed. Seedy people don't look successful, and no one wants to hire someone who looks other than successful. Breakfast toast crumbs in the corner of your mouth, dandruff flakes on your shoulders, or a slightly soiled shirt or blouse can make an irreversible bad impression on the person who has the power to hire you or reject you. John T. Molloy, a wardrobe consultant to many corporations, has two books on the subject of appearance: *Dress for Success* (for men) and *The Woman's Dress for Success Book*.

It's important to give the impression that you understand that the interviewer's time is valuable. Be on time for your interview. Conversely, you should establish (without having a chip on your shoulder) that your time is every bit as valuable. It would be a mistake to be too early for your interview. His or her secretary will probably announce you, and if unoccupied, the executive will probably see you early. But you may leave the impression that you were somewhat overeager. Overeager applicants are sometimes suspect. So if you find that the highways were not as crowded as you had anticipated or that for any reason you're in the vicinity with time to kill, kill that time. It's better to walk around the block a few times and appear at the designated time.

Meet your interviewer with a positive attitude. Each of you has something the other person wants. He or she has a job to offer you. You have the ability to fill that job ably and thus make him or her look good. The person who hires you lays his or her reputation on the line. It's up to you, by word and manner, to make the interviewer confident that you're going to make him or her look good.

You are announced, ushered into the interviewer's office, and introduced. Go slowly here. The wrong move could set the tone for the entire interview. Don't automatically take a chair. Wait a moment, and if you aren't invited to sit down, ask permission. That's just a small detail, but some interviewers are sensitive to manifestations of assumptiveness or arrogance.

Smoking is a more sensitive consideration. With all the evidence of the harmful effects of smoking and the possibility that smoke from someone else's cigarette negatively affects nonsmokers in the same room, you would be risking offending your interviewer if you even asked permission to smoke. Even if he or she disliked cigarette smoke violently, it would be awkward to refuse someone the courtesy when asked. But he or she may resent you. So don't ask. The only condition under which you would be justified to light up is if your interviewer invited you to do so.

What if he or she smokes and you don't? Don't be a militant. Your interviewer is in the driver's seat. There will be time later, if you start work there, to say that you would prefer your office space to be away from cigarette smoke.

**APPEAL TO THE
COMPANY'S SELF-INTEREST**

After the preliminary amenities have been taken care of, the interviewer generally will describe the opening and the type of person needed to fill it. Sometimes you'll even get a selling pitch on what a great company it is to work for. Don't allow this to make you overconfident and feel that you have the job—the interviewer probably has said the very same thing to every other applicant.

Let the interviewer set the pace and do most of the talking. Answer questions thoughtfully, without shooting from the lip. But don't hesitate too long; that would make you appear uncertain and indecisive. If you're not sure of the question, ask for clarification. Don't answer a question that he or she didn't ask.

Be specific in all your answers, slanting them toward the job you're after. Try to make it very clear that you can do a great job for the company. Remember that the basis of this interview is to establish what you can do for them, not what they can do for you. This half-hour or so means a lot more to you than to your interviewer. This is the most important thing on your agenda for the day, while he or she has had to put aside primary duties and assignments in order to devote this time to you.

There will inevitably come a point in the interview when it appears that almost everything has been covered. There may even be a bit of what broadcast people call "dead-air space." This would be a good time for you to take the ball and run with it.

Paul Norsell believes this can be advantageous to the applicant if handled right. "Not everyone is adept at interviewing," he said, "so the applicant can help by explaining why he feels he can benefit the employer. But you must use discretion. A two-minute answer to a question that could be answered with a yes or no could easily turn off an interviewer."

Herb Moss said, "If there's silence, it's a good idea to fill it judiciously. Be prepared with a brief synopsis of your accomplishments. But don't box yourself in by mentioning money unless your interviewer does first."

Paul Norsell had this to say: "The company should be the one to extend an offer of money, based on the level of the job, your background, and so forth."

BE RELAXED
BUT NOT TOO RELAXED

Guard against being too much at ease. You don't want to brag or to confide. Be wary of the interviewer who asks you to start by telling him or her about yourself. If you're faced with such a request, it is wise to ask for some more specific direction, such as, "Shall I give you a rundown on my responsibilities on my last job?"

Be persuasive when you are talking, confident but not boastful. If your interviewer appears to be argumentative, avoid any confrontation. If he or she turns out to be a bully, don't fight back. You just cannot win.

Another no-win situation is to bad-mouth your last employer. Never do it under any circumstance. Everyone knows that good people often are fired. Let it be assumed that this is what happened. The more you protest, the more you appear to be the culpable party.

EXPECT THE THIRD DEGREE

Some interviewers conduct their sessions like detectives questioning suspects in the precinct interrogation room. That's their prerogative, as long as you're coming to them. Usually it's a tactic, and they're not nearly as mean as they seem. You can turn this to your advantage by keeping cool. Perhaps the job has extraordinary pressures, and the interview is being used to determine an applicant's ability to keep his or her head when things get tense.

Sometimes, especially for a high-echelon opening, a couple of top executives may "double-team" an applicant. This happened to me once. I was given a chair in the middle, facing two high-powered executives who sat about 60 degrees on each side of me. They fired rapid questions, taking turns and never revealing their reactions to my answers. Some of the questions were about how I might handle certain advertising and marketing problems for their largest client. My answer for this type of question was, "I wouldn't presume to give you a recommendation on that without knowing more about the state of the market and your client's position versus the competition." That was the first and only time they cracked smiles, and I knew I'd said just the right thing. I got the job.

Be prepared to answer some very incisive questions, and even some bordering on the personal. Don't ever get hot under the collar, even if you feel you must say, "I don't think I should have to answer questions such as that." But say it with a smile, and you're usually home free. If your refusal to answer is held against you, so be it. It could mean that this is not the place for you to be spending your business life.

Here are some questions you may be expected to answer on the spur of the moment:

- Why did you leave your last job? (We've gone over this one in chapter three. To reiterate, the

truth is the only way to go. Let the chips fall
where they may.)
- Would it be all right with you if we phoned your
ex-boss? (Your answer should be, "Yes, of course."
If you anticipate a bad reference, see the section
"How to neutralize a bad reference" in this
chapter.)
- What have you been doing since then?
- Would you describe yourself as a healthy person?
- If you had to characterize yourself in one sentence,
what would you say? (This is a real beartrap of a
question. I answered it once with "If I was able to
characterize myself in just one sentence, you'd
never want to hire me!" When I said it, the man
broke into a grin, and it set a wonderful tone for
the rest of the interview.)
- Could you give me your strongest and weakest
points? (Another loaded question. One way to
answer it is to give your strong points first. Then
say that you've identified a couple of weak points
and that you're well on the road to correcting
them. If he or she wants to know what they are,
tell what the weaknesses are, and at the same time,
tell how you're working on them.)
- Is there a particular type of work you dislike very
much?
- Never mind what job is open now. If you had your
druthers, which job in this company would you
prefer? (Another possible trap. You could say that
you aren't fully acquainted with all the opportunities in the company, but that the job you are going
after seems to be a good starting point. This way
you avoid exhibiting delusions of grandeur.)
- Do you have any hangups about working for a
woman? (If you do, better do something about

them. The odds of having a female boss get shorter
by the year.)
- Would you mind working for someone younger
than you?

These are just some of the more common questions
you may expect to have fired at you. Be prepared and
stay loose.

HOW TO HANDLE BEING OVERQUALIFIED

Somewhere in the course of the interview, it may be
suggested that you are overqualified for the job. This can
be a gentle hint that you are either too old or too high-
priced.

There is a way to overcome this line of thinking. Your
age can be turned into an advantage. It can mean that
you're highly experienced and that you work with confidence and without false starts. The chances are that you
get the job done faster and get it done right the first time.
There's less chance that it will cost the employer money
to train you, so there is an immediate return on the investment in you.

Make it clear that you know it entails a considerable
investment in training time every time someone new is
hired, and that, in your case, most of this has already
been paid for by past employers. So your depth of experience is a bonus the company gets when they hire you.
Sure you cost more per year than a younger person who
may be untried and in need of training. But you're worth
it. Not only that, but you're in excellent health and
haven't missed a day's work in a long while.

HOW TO NEUTRALIZE A BAD REFERENCE

Will Rogers once said, "I never met a man I didn't
like." Unfortunately, few of us could say the same. The

rough-and-tumble of everyday business life makes for bruised egos, imaginary and real injustices, and people who simply cannot get along with certain other people. It could be because of bad chemistry or any number of other reasons.

Someone somewhere in your past probably dislikes you. It usually doesn't matter much, unless that someone is asked for his or her assessment of you as a potential employee. Then it can be a problem.

It isn't enough simply to overlook that person's name when you're asked for references, especially if he or she had a prominent role in your business life. Some companies make a point of seeking out people who aren't mentioned by the candidate, especially if it is likely that they might have worked closely with the applicant.

If you have someone such as this in your past, lay it on the line. You can say something like this: "In all the years I've been in this industry, there's only one person I've worked with who probably would give you a very negative opinion of me. I'll give you that name. But I'd also like you to talk with another person in the same department, so as to get a balanced opinion of my contribution to the company." No need to explain why you didn't get along—it happens all the time. What will probably happen is that the interviewer will end up getting more than two opinions from that firm. Or, respecting your candor, he or she may not bother checking out that company at all.

THE CEREMONIAL INTERVIEW

One of the mixed blessings you're bound to encounter during your search is the interview you're granted as a favor. It may be a direct favor to you or to a close friend of yours. Perhaps you have a friend in a high position in a company. He or she may not have an opening but wants to help in some way. An interview for the record seems to be a good way. Or perhaps a friend intercedes with an influential executive.

The result of the ceremonial interview is usually very fuzzy. You may have made an excellent impression on a person who isn't in a position to do much about it. This may lead to your being sent to another friend, and the beat goes on. Lightning may strike, but the odds are heavily against it.

How do you handle the ceremonial interview? You can't just turn down all these well-meaning friends. One way to handle this situation is to make it clear at the interview that you don't intend to ask for a job but that you could use some counsel. For example, you can say, "As you may know, most of my experience is in the frammus industry. I've always felt I could do a job for So-and-So Company. What would be your advice as a good way to approach the people there?"

Now the ceremonial interviewer is really at ease; he or she doesn't have to be on guard to fend you off. And you are relaxed, too. You're not asking for the moon, just for some good advice and help, which is flattering to most people.

At best you may get a letter of introduction or the promise of an advance telephone call to someone at So-and-So Company. This gives you an immediate advantage, getting you around the personnel department and the outer defenses of receptionists and secretaries, right into the office of the decision maker. This is just one way to turn the ceremonial interview into a fruitful contact.

Here's another way. If you are very sure that there's an actual opening in the interviewer's company, you may say this: "I don't want to take up too much of your time. But since I've heard there's an opening I believe I can fill, would you be willing to introduce me to the person responsible for the hiring of the new employee?" Again you've managed to get past the outer ring of defenses.

It has been estimated that three quarters of the total market for white collar jobs is "hidden." That is, the openings are never advertised or put into the hands of employment specialists. Therefore, the more insiders who know of your abilities and availability, the greater the chance that you'll be thought of in connection with one of those hidden jobs. The hidden job market is discussed more extensively in the next chapter.

QUIT WHILE YOU'RE AHEAD

There are no statistics on how many people talk themselves out of jobs that were already theirs. But if things are going well with your interview, you may have a tendency to let down your guard. The time to be friendly with your interviewer is after you're a member in good standing and have no axe to grind.

Get a feel of when the interview should end. After you've stated your case and the interviewer has had a chance to fully explore your credentials, it's time to stop. If the interview is lagging, and if the interviewer is finding it hard to wind it up, look at your watch and say, "I don't want to take up any more of your time now. I'd be happy to come back if you want me to add to what we've discussed or to see someone else." Then get up, shake hands, thank your interviewer, and leave. Be sure to write a thank-you note. Someone has taken time out of his or her busy day to see you, and that's worth a thanks.

10

Other
Door-Openers

There are outside companies and agencies, either private or run by the government, that make it their business to find people for jobs. If you are interested, there are also firms that will package you for potential employers. And there's the "hidden job market" to be tapped.

EXECUTIVE SEARCH FIRMS

You're undoubtedly aware of the executive search firms, often called "headhunters," "body snatchers," or "flesh peddlers." Usually, these firms are hired by companies, organizations, or branches of government to search for key personnel. The firms work for their clients on either a retainer contract or a fee-paid basis, and as you may expect, they serve the interest of their clients, not your interests.

Executive search firms generally do not solicit resumes or applications from job hunters. However, part of the research material the firms use consists of files of resumes, cross-indexed by type of work or endeavor. The resumes are used as source material for prospects at the time assignments are received from the clients.

Many of the personnel leads these firms get come from people they know and trust. Executive recruiters also do a great deal of research and cold calling on management in specific industries they wish to specialize in. This way, the recruiters provide themselves with prospects and leads for future openings. For example, if an executive search firm is on a retainer contract to supply candidates to General Motors, you can bet that recruiters from that firm will be beating the bushes in Detroit on a regular basis. They'll find out who the good automotive people are and who may be susceptible to a good offer.

It's possible that your name is already on the list of an executive search firm. In addition, some of your friends and colleagues may have contacts with executive recruiters and may feed your name to them. Others of your colleagues may be contacted by search firms and asked to recommend candidates. Your name may come up.

You can also make the contact yourself. You may have the impression that most search firms are interested only in placing people who already hold good jobs, and that they seldom, if ever, are interested in the unemployed. That's dead wrong. Herb Moss says, "Many unemployed people are victims of circumstances, mergers, acquisitions, personality clashes, and so on. Good people, even though unemployed, are of interest to the executive search consultant if he or she has a client assignment in the person's field."

Paul Norsell also expressed interest in placing good unemployed people. "It's a common misunderstanding that executive search companies aren't interested," he said. "We're highly selective. We want to send the best possible candidates to our clients. If a person is unemployed yet highly qualified, we would propose him or her to any of our clients."

I asked him how he felt about dealing with a person who had been fired. "Depends on the cause," Mr. Norsell said. "If it was an integrity problem or bad judgment, it would be difficult to place the individual. But if the cause of firing was something such as bad chemistry, which is often real, the situation is easier."

Both Herb Moss and Paul Norsell said they welcome unsolicited resumes. "The recruiter works for the company," Mr. Moss said, "and wants to cover the entire spectrum so as to furnish the best candidate. We use our cross-reference files regularly. I'd advise any unemployed executive to send a resume with a brief covering letter to any executive search firms specializing in his or her field."

If you are ever contacted by an executive search firm, don't appear overeager. Express sincere interest, if indeed you are interested. But play it cool. Remember that these firms are accustomed to wooing people who already hold down good jobs and who have normal and understandable reservations, at least at the outset.

Another thing to keep in mind about an executive search firm is that they are paid to find the right man or woman for an opening. A firm tries to send several candidates to a client. The only criterion from the client is that each applicant is outstanding. The reputation of the search firm rides on that requirement. If you are lucky enough to be sent out on a job interview by an executive search firm, you should feel very good about it. The people there think you're someone special. And they're paid to be right!

Having an executive search firm interested in you costs nothing at all, and it gives you a very good chance of shortening your job-hunting period. Find out which ones are the best in your field and send them your resume.

EMPLOYMENT AGENCIES

Now let's examine the regular licensed employment agencies, the type that usually advertise in the classified pages of daily and Sunday newspapers. These firms are on a completely different wavelength than are the executive search firms. They generally operate on a per-job basis. Oftentimes, an agency does not have exclusive access to a particular job.

Like executive recruiters, employment agency personnel are in the business of finding people for jobs, not jobs for people. The way the agency people see it, you only come to them once, while hopefully their client keeps coming back with more job openings. So you know where the loyalties of the agency lie.

You should consider the fact that more than one employment agency may be listing an identical opening and sending out people to interview for the job. It's perfectly legal. However, if you were to get a lead from two or three about the same opening and were then to land the job, a messy dispute over who told you about it first could result.

Herbert Moss stated, "If you are going to use employment agencies, I believe you should register with three or four of the best. Occasionally, one may send you out on the same job as another agency. But they generally work for different corporate clients. Therefore, your chances or choices are increased. Unfortunately, there are many second-rate agencies, a waste of the job seeker's time."

The key is to find first-rate employment agencies, the kind that are willing to work with you. Your employment counselor should market your talents intelligently and only send you out on interviews that have a reasonable chance of being successful. In a manner of speaking, you are the salesperson for the employment agent. If he or she is careful, only one salesperson should have to be sent out to make any one sale. Some agents send several job hunters out for the same opening. This kind of intramural competition you don't need. If you discover that this sort of thing is happening, perhaps it's time to change employment agencies.

When asked for her views on multiple referrals, Pamela Reeve, who runs Pamela Reeve Agency in Beverly Hills, California, replied, "If an employer receives a quantity of resumes from an undiscerning agent, he or she doesn't know where to start interviewing. And if there are losers in the batch, you will be put into the same category. This mass sending of resumes and applicants is better known as the 'buckshot approach.'

"Also, if an agent sends your resume around to numerous employers when there are no jobs available or when the job is wrong for you, your name is flooded into the market. Then, when the 'real' job comes along, you tend to lose your bargaining power."

Most good employment agencies get their fees from the companies who assign them to furnish applicants. They usually don't even try to hold the applicant liable. There are, however, variant firms who call themselves "placement agencies." These people may ask you to sign an agreement that if the employer won't pay the fee, you will. Don't sign.

If the company wants you, it should be willing to pick up the fee. It's a cinch that your new employer can afford the fee better than you can. Most employers automatically pay the fee. Get it straight when you register that you want the fee paid by the firm that hires you. If you're asked to fill out an application form at the placement agency, be sure it doesn't include a contract. And be especially careful of the fine print.

ASK UNCLE

The United States Employment Service is tied in with the various state employment services, which are in turn affiliated with the unemployment insurance program. Before you receive unemployment insurance, you are required to have an interview with a specialist in your field at your state employment service office. Depending on your salary level and number of years of experience, there may be some very good openings the counselors can send you after.

If you're above the $20,000 salary level, the interview will probably be more of a formality. Most of the jobs in the files are lower-level ones, and the state employment offices do an outstanding job of filling them. Large companies usually communicate their employee requirements there. Many of the local employment service offices have computerized job banks and are continuously storing new information about openings.

I've been interviewed by state employment service counselors three different times. Each time a very pleasant person would finally tell me that I was overqualified for any of the advertising openings and that rarely was there anything in my bracket. I was asked to call back in a month. I said thanks and left. A month later, the situation wouldn't have changed.

Since it's necessary to go through the motions in order to be eligible for your unemployment insurance, you'll have to complete this interview. You may be pleasantly surprised.

CAREER PREPARATION
AND GUIDANCE FIRMS

This is an entirely different category. Firms advertise under this heading attempting to attract job hunters. These firms rarely, if ever, have openings to fill. Rather they claim to be specialists in grooming people to find jobs. These places offer, for what may be a very stiff fee, to teach you how to open doors, get important interviews, handle yourself, gain personal insights, intensify your goals, market your capabilities, and so forth. The first interview usually is a confidential, no-obligation session. During this time, you will be asked to sign up for their services.

Some of their advertising appeals run along these lines: "Going nowhere? We can help you"; "Let our specialists help you discover the hidden job market"; "Most good jobs are not advertised"; and so on. The tip-off for you is that this type of organization must use a disclaimer in their ads. It usually reads, "Not an employment agency or job-placement agency. Fee for professional services," or "Not an offer of employment—fee for professional services."

When, if ever, should a person decide to use the services of this type of organization? Only you can answer that. It would appear to be a luxury with a very high risk of not paying off. Many of the services offered are things that any mature, analytical person would soon figure out. In fact, most of the discussion we've had thus far in this book is directed toward helping you do it yourself, thus saving such a fee. Even if you did engage the help of such a firm, in the final analysis, it's still up to you.

So why not do your own spadework? In doing it, you'll develop the self-confidence and assurance that you'll need when the job is on the line. A friend of mine signed with one of these career preparation and guidance firms several years ago. According to him, he felt as though he was being maneuvered like a puppet on strings. He became nervous and tense—not ideal job-hunting characteristics. Eventually he disengaged himself and attempted to get a refund. The last time I talked with him, he was wondering if he could afford to sue.

One incident doesn't mean that all these organizations are the same. Perhaps there's one that could add some magic to your job search, even shorten the time span. But my advice would be to give it an all-out effort yourself before you call in the Marines.

THE HIDDEN JOB MARKET

Many employment professionals estimate that about three fourths of all job openings above the clerical and labor levels never get publicized. Most of these are filled by personal recommendations, people who are known to be good prospects by someone inside the company; by people who have applied previously and are on hold; by people promoted from within; by people who time their applications fortuitously; and by people sent in by executive search companies that have instant candidates on tap.

Many jobs are never officially open. People within the company have advance notice that someone is retiring or leaving. The opening may be weeks or months in the future, so there's no need for advertising or calling in a recruiter or employment agency. The word gets out informally, and often several good candidates are interviewed long before the opening exists.

Recognizing this hidden job market, it becomes clear that you should never stop your personal job search, no matter how many outside people you consult. Your energy, optimism, good judgment, and demonstrated talent are the best combination of reasons why someone should be happy to hire you.

How do you get into this huge hidden job market? You've already taken the most important step if you've spread the word to your friends and acquaintances that you're looking for a job. They're going to be "bird-dogging" for you every time they see a job posted on the company bulletin board. Your friends will think of you the moment word gets out that someone is retiring, being transferred, or otherwise leaving. If a new department is being formed, a new sales district established, or any other opening created, you'll probably be tipped off. So the smartest thing you can do is to keep in constant touch with your contacts in any company you'd like to join. It can make all the difference.

11

"Honey, You've Got a Real Problem!"

In the last chapter, we discussed the various types of outside agencies you can use to help you get those all-important interviews. Some are worthwhile, and some are hardly worth the time, trouble, and sometimes money.

If you decide to go the executive-recruitment or employment-agency route, watch out for the bruising of your ego or even the shattering of your confidence It could happen if you're unlucky enough to meet up with an insensitive counselor in one of those agencies.

The first time I was fired, with all the resultant trauma, I had the great misfortune to run into a boorish counselor who temporarily destroyed me. Talk about being vulnerable—I was that. From vice-president and creative director of the large Los Angeles office of a national advertising agency, making an excellent salary, I was thrown suddenly onto the job market in a city I barely knew, with very few contacts. After six months of beating my head against a brick wall, I was granted an interview with the most successful headhunter in advertising on the west coast for a job that sounded terrific. A well-meaning friend had helped me out.

For the sake of anonymity, I'll call her Ginny Gordon. I'd like to share this experience with you, if only to prove that you're not alone with your feelings.

I had an eleven o'clock appointment with Ginny Gordon. It was a lovely spring day. The Dodgers were due to play the Cardinals at Chavez Ravine in a few hours, one of their infrequent afternoon games. I might have taken the afternoon off to see the game, using the company box. But now I had no company.

I was so nervous, my stomach was turning. Ginny Gordon's offices were in one of those flimsy glass-and-steel buildings that you find on every other corner in West Hollywood. Some buildings are full of agents and business managers; others have film or sound studios. All look like a Hollywood set for a big-business movie.

On my way in, I ducked into the washroom, making sure my proofbook rested on a dry spot on the tile floor. Then I splashed cold water on my face to restore that fresh, ruddy look.

My hair was something else, though. I looked in the mirror, then combed my hair over the bald spot on top. "I really have a fairly good head of hair," I thought. "If it wasn't for the gray in the sideburns, I could maybe pass for thirty-five. Plenty of guys ten years younger have more gray than me. Next time, I'll tell Sal to go a little closer with the clippers."

Other than that, I looked pretty sharp and in very good shape. Perhaps a tad too well groomed. I wished I could have been a bit more careless about this job hunting. But when you don't really feel that way inside, you can't fake it. At least, I couldn't. I needed that job badly, and that was the plain truth.

Her offices were furnished in Danish modern, so new and slick they were intimidating. Most of the employment agencies looked like warehouses—dusty and grim, with battered furniture and the lowest possible overhead. This woman had the look of success and a corner on most of the good jobs. Also, from what I'd heard, she had the arrogance to go with it. Hards as nails and brutally candid, my friend warned me. So my guard was up.

I told the receptionist my name. "I have an eleven o'clock appointment with Miss Gordon. I'm a little early. . . ."

"Wait out there," the receptionist interrupted, indicating a waiting area. I hated myself for the apologetic tinge I put in my voice. That was what being out of work for six months had done to me. My palms began to sweat.

I must have hesitated. The receptionist said, "She's tied up for a while. Meantime, you can fill out our forms." I was handed a four-page application.

I was so sick of filling out those forms! "All of this information is in my resume," I said.

"Sorry," she answered, as if she were programmed, "but we need this for our files." I pulled up a chair and started writing. I'd filled out so many applications lately that I could have done this one with my eyes closed. The door was still closed when I finished. I sat back and tried to relax.

Finally the inner door swung open. The receptionist smiled for the first time, probably aware that her boss was watching. "Miss Gordon will see you now," she told me, overly polite.

The woman in the office didn't square up with what I had expected. She appeared more sympathetic and courteous than described.

She glanced up, and my first impression went down

the tube. She seemed to look right through me. "Close the door, honey, will you?" Her voice was clipped.

I obeyed automatically. She had to be fifteen years younger than me, but I was acting like a kid in school.

She indicated a chair at the side of her desk. "Please have a seat."

I stumbled over myself getting seated. I leaned my proofbook and attaché case against her desk.

"May I call you Jerry?" she asked.

I nodded. "Certainly."

She looked at, and through, me again. "Now, which job was it that you were after?"

I wondered if perhaps she did know and was just playing games. "Creative director—west coast branch of large eastern agency. You advertised it in this week's *MAC* [*Media Agencies Clients*]."

Her eyes flicked upwards, taking in my hair and everything else. "How old did you say you were?" (Today she probably would not dare to ask that one.)

"I didn't say." Score one for the old pro. I'd been thrusting and parrying way back when she was playing with building blocks. But I picked up the slack before she had a chance to feel taken. "Here's my resume. I'm forty-one with twenty years experience in the top agencies." I handed it over. I'd shaved four years off my age, but I've always looked younger.

She gave it a quick glance. "With a track record like this, you shouldn't have any trouble at all. How long have you been looking?"

It was the question they always asked. My throat tightened, and I was afraid I might sound as tense as I felt. "Six months."

The atmosphere in her office chilled noticeably. "Nothing in between?"

"Nothing I'd seriously consider. I've made as much as forty thousand, and now they're talking fifteen."

She sat, giving me the top-to-bottom once-over. She didn't miss a thing, from my fresh shoeshine to the gray in my sideburns. When she finally spoke, she sounded like a manuscript rejection slip on tape. "I wouldn't be fair to you if I wasn't completely candid, would I?"

"Go ahead," I said, straining to keep my voice level. I couldn't let the bitterness come through, despite the six months of turndowns.

"Honey," she said, and her familiarity was beginning to grate on me, "you've got a real problem. No question about it."

I hadn't killed an entire morning just to have someone tell me that. But I was running out of options, so I let her run off at the mouth.

"I could place you in a number of copy spots, but none of them pay over ten," she said. "And even then, they're always looking for the young turk who might come up with the big idea."

"What's a young turk?" I asked.

She shrugged. "They seem to think it's the bright young kid with ideas sprouting out of the ears."

"And cheap, too, I'll bet!" I said.

She smiled. "That might have more than a little to do with it!"

I liked her a little better. "What about that opening for a creative director?"

She shook her head. "I'm afraid you don't fit their specs for that job."

I could have asked her what their specs were, but I was pretty sure I already knew. So I didn't ask, and she knew why I didn't. Yet I couldn't help bursting out with, "Since when does a guy have to be under thirty to come up with the big idea?"

"I never believed that fiction," she said. A soft answer turneth away wrath.

"Well, someone must be perpetuating the myth," I

said. "But I want you to know that I've been coming up with the big idea all my business life. All you have to do is look at my work."

"Let's do it, then," she said.

I showed her my best magazine proofs first. Beer, automobile, and cake mix. All four-color stuff, a bit dogeared from too much handling.

"Very nice," she said carefully. "But how about something contemporary, maybe in the past year or so?"

The same words and music. "Well, as I mentioned, I haven't been working the past six months. And some of the copy I had to write for my last client, I wouldn't show to my worst enemy."

"I see." But I wasn't sure she really did. "How's your reel?" she then asked.

"Good," I said.

"Anything current?"

"Same situation," I had to say. "Some storyboards and scripts I'm rather pleased with. But nothing good got onto film recently."

She shook her head. "Well, I did say you had a problem, Jerry. We'll work along with you, but I can't offer much encouragement right at the moment. Things are tight, and they all seem to be looking for kids. Cheap talent. Now, if you were under thirty, and maybe even a minority, I could place you in any one of five jobs, paying up to fifteen thousand. And that's with a minimum of copywriting experience. Just as long as there's latent writing ability there." She looked me straight in the eye. "Unfair, isn't it?"

Suddenly I wasn't tense any more. Just angry. "Unfair, hell! It's a dishonest, filthy mess!" Now that I'd gotten it off my chest, I was starting to like her.

Ginny spread her palms helplessly. "Maybe it's different in New York or Chicago. But this is how it is in Los Angeles. I only fill the orders."

The phone rang. She motioned for me to stay put while she answered it. "Yes, speaking." Pause. "Under thirty, black, and you'll go to fifteen?" Another pause. "I wish I could. Not a single one in my files. Are you sure it has to be? . . ." She grimaced at me. "Yes, I'll let you know the minute I get one." She hung up and looked at me quizzically. "Any questions?" And, for what it was worth, I knew that she knew the kind of hell I was going through.

I started laughing. Nothing hysterical, mind you. Just a good, rib-aching laugh that made me feel better. "No questions. You levelled with me, and I thank you for that." I crammed my proofs into the envelope.

She walked me to the door. "I'm sorry I couldn't be of more help. Honestly."

"Thanks, anyway," I said.

"We'll keep your resume on file, that goes without saying. But don't count on a thing."

"Right now, I wouldn't count on my mother, Uncle Sam, or even apple pie. Thanks again."

I crossed Sunset Boulevard and walked back to my car. Was this really happening to me? In Chicago I would have had at least half a dozen offers by now. The phone was always ringing back there. Someone either wanting something or offering something. Give and take. You scratch my back, and I'll scratch yours. Phony, maybe. But it was living. By comparison, this was a slow death.

I couldn't believe my watch—only eleven-thirty. I'd allowed a full hour for Ginny Gordon, and now I had time on my hands. There were some phone calls I knew I should make. But it wasn't too good an idea to phone any of my prospects this close to lunch. You never knew how someone would react when in a hurry to get out for lunch—cranky, perhaps, and more likely to give me the brush-off. With too few good leads remaining, there was no point in jeopardizing any of them.

I started driving aimlessly—south on Doheny to Burton Way, then east on Third. The next thing I knew, I was parked in the Farmers' Market lot, my group therapy. I walked among the stalls, taking in the colors of the beautiful fruits and vegetables, the good smells of tacos, fresh peanut butter, roasting coffee, walnut fudge, and fried clams. I looked into all the carefree faces of the tourists from places that weren't supposed to have the things we're blessed with out here. But most of them seemed so happy.

Two youngsters sat at a table in the courtyard. They must have been about eighteen or nineteen, both in jeans, letting their food get cold while they smiled at one another. What if I went up and touched them, one with my right hand, one with my left? Would some of their magic flow into me like a current of electricity, some of their eagerness and optimism?

All of a sudden, I felt terribly tired and alone. I walked slowly back to my car and drove home.

That day had to be one of the lowest points of my job hunt. Remember, it was the first time, and I had fallen a long way. Obviously, I recovered and went on to better days. I share this episode with you so that you can be prepared to cope with similar feelings and happenings. And so that you'll realize you're not alone.

12

The Acid Test
of Friendship

When you're out of work, everyone you've ever considered to be your friend will, at one time or another, be given the acid test. This is another of the ordeals you'll be forced to go through. I can almost guarantee that you'll suffer a certain amount of disillusionment. Conversely, you'll have your spirits lifted by kindnesses from some unexpected sources.

When I first got started in the business world, fresh out of my World War II uniform, I was fortunate to be working for a kind, pragmatic individual. At the time, I thought he was rather cold and abrupt. But at the oddest moments, he would take the time to pass along to me small pieces of priceless advice. Most of them have stood the test of time very well. One that has always stayed in my mind is: "Don't expect to collect a large number of friends. If in the course of your entire lifetime you can count the number of true friends you have on the fingers of one hand, you're a very lucky person."

Think about that for a moment. I'm not referring to the gossip column items wherein some movie star is quoted as throwing a party for "a few hundred of my closest friends." I mean real friends, the kind you can always count on when things are going poorly.

No one would dispute the fact that friends help to enrich our lives, which brings me to one of the very few bright spots of being out of work—you get to find out who your real friends are. This is so true that it's trite. Yet it happens every time.

Why is it that so many people reveal themselves to be shallow, unfeeling, and devoid of any real character once they've discovered that someone who had occupied a seat of some power is no longer able to wield it? Very soon, you'll discover that they never really were your friends. It was your position of power that they were friends with. You were the one who held the ability to make something happen for them. So you were catered to, apple-polished, flattered, wined, and dined. Suddenly, in their minds, you've been transformed into a nonentity. So they're off and running, looking for the next person who may be able to do them some good.

You see these types at parties, conventions, and meetings. Just try to lock eyes with them while they're shaking hands with you. It's darned near impossible. You see, they're usually looking over your shoulder to see whether perhaps someone with more clout is within hailing distance.

A friend of mine used to be the president of a large retail organization. He was a highly principled man with a great sense of loyalty. I'll call him Steve.

Steve's firm was bought out by a large conglomerate, and he was ordered to fire one of his able assistants. When he flatly refused to do so, the hatchet man for the parent company flew across the country to fire both the assistant and my friend, the president.

It's debatable whether Steve's courageous stand was worth it, since he was left out on a limb with no maneuvering room at all. If he had played it cool, he could have looked around and jumped laterally. As it was, he was out in the cold and in very sore straits. He was just not accustomed to this manner of treatment, because he had never treated others this way.

During the very lowest period of his unemployment, his wife confided to us about her bitter disillusionment. "We never had to worry about vacations and trips. There was always someone inviting us somewhere. Now we don't go anywhere. And when Steve decided to attend the convention last month in Las Vegas, some of those ex-friends looked at us as though they didn't even recognize us! These were the same people who used to send around their limousines to pick us up for their parties! This time no one even invited us to a hospitality suite. So we bought all of our drinks at the hotel bar."

My friend and his wife were hurt deeply by all of this. Their mistake was that they had been deluded into thinking that all the kowtowing in the past was based on deep friendships rather than on how many dozen items his buyer might order the next time.

If Steve had prepared himself for this kind of cruel, unfeeling rejection, it wouldn't have hurt him and his wife nearly as much as it did. So you be ready for it. Tell yourself that it's really nothing personal. Because it never was anything personal.

There are some other petty cruelties you must be ready for, such as phoning someone who knows very well who you are and drawing a blank. It could happen any number of ways. Perhaps the secretary comes back on the phone with "What did you say your name was?"; "May I ask what this call is in regard to?"; "What company are you with?"; "Mr. Smith suggests you write him a letter"; "Is there something I can help you with?"; "Can you speak with anyone else in the firm?"; or "She's in a meeting right now," which could be true the first few times, but not after the fifth phone call, when you've left your own number each time. Or you may be told, "He's out of town and won't be back until a week from Monday," to be followed a week from Monday with the "he's in a meeting" lie and finally with "Can you speak with someone else?" Just about that time, no matter how thick your skin is, you begin to get the message loud and clear.

Treatment such as this from people you thought liked you can make the most secure individual feel bitter and more than slightly paranoid. But keep telling yourself that it has nothing to do with you personally. Some people get a perverse thrill out of making a jobless person squirm. When they were kids, they probably kicked dogs, set fire to cats, or picked the wings from butterflies. They get a warm feeling out of savoring the fact that they're safe and snug on a payroll and you aren't. The more people they kick, the luckier they feel that no one can do that to them—yet.

Bide your time. You're going to be back on the job very soon. And it's highly probable that some of these nasty individuals will be out pounding the pavement sooner or later. They may even start to remember you again. And that's just the time you may start to forget them. Few can begrudge you that small triumph of retribution.

So far this chapter has probably made you feel rather rotten. Sadly enough, that's the way life can often be. But there is another side to the coin—the kindnesses you may receive from completely strange and unexpected sources. How can this be? I guess the answer is that for every boor in the world, there must be at least one warm, friendly, caring human being. Perhaps even more. People of this sort usually show up just when things are looking their darkest. Let me tell you about how it happened to me.

Up to this point, I've avoided using any real names. But I'm going to make an exception in this case. It happened when I was at absolute rock bottom in my search for a new job. I'd been out of work for seven months and was digging much too deeply into our savings. I saw an ad in the *Los Angeles Times* that, under normal circumstances, I never would have given a second look. *Reader's Digest* was looking for a merchandising person.

This is generally a job for a young person not long out of college. He or she travels around to retail outlets and shows the managers what is being advertised currently in the magazine, doing his or her best to convince these people that it will be profitable for them to feature and push these products during the month. It paid probably about one third of what I'd been earning in my last job. But it was a job, and I needed one badly. So I answered the ad.

Two days later, my phone rang. "Hello, is this Jerry Cowle?" said the pleasant voice at the other end. "Look, fella, my name's Frank Rice—from the *Reader's Digest*. You answered our ad for the merchandising job. I'm looking at your resume right now."

"Oh, yes!" I said, perking up.

"I don't think it's the right job for you," Frank Rice said. My heart sank.

"You're much too good for something like that," he continued, and suddenly my spirits lifted. "Look, Jerry, you're a heavyweight creative man. There has to be a job in town that's right for your talents. This is a very impressive resume!"

"I know it is," I said. "But, to tell you the truth, Mr. Rice, I'd take just about anything in the way of a job at this point."

"Don't do it!" he said. "Hold out. Listen, I'd like to

help you. Fellows in my spot get to meet a lot of nice people in our business. I have to believe that one of them could use a talent like yours. How about meeting me for lunch today, and we can talk it over?"

We met at his club—an opulent place called Cave des Roys. Frank turned out to be a handsome, personable man who made me feel at ease immediately. Before we even got around to ordering lunch, he'd learned more about me than any of the people who'd interviewed me. He made me feel like a top-notch advertising man who had been tragically overlooked by a shortsighted industry that was in reality starving for people like me. It was all too true. But I'd long ago lost sight of it until that red-letter day.

For two hours, I was treated with a degree of kindness and warmth that I had almost forgotten existed. And Frank didn't let it rest there. He followed up—calling a number of people, setting up appointments for me, and helping me to raise my sights once more.

It would make a beautiful wrap-up to this story if I could say that one of the leads Frank gave me turned out to be the one that landed me my next job. It didn't work out exactly that way. But it might as well have. Because Frank's extended hand of friendship nourished my soul and morale at a time when all seemed bleak and hopeless. I hope you're fortunate enough to meet someone like Frank when you sorely need a friend.

13

Don't Let
the Doldrums
Stop You

"In a few weeks," you told yourself (and anyone else near and dear to you), "the word will get around in the trade. Then I'll have a potful of offers to choose from." And you believed it!

You weren't merely whistling past the graveyard. You figured that when the news got around in the industry, all the people who had been burned by your expertise in the past would be trying to corral you for the rival company. You expected to hear from the people who tried for years to lure you away from XYZ Corporation. After all, you turned down plenty of offers over the years just to stay at your job. And it turned out that loyalty wasn't a two-way street. You were going to show them at XYZ that you were still in big demand, even if they let you go.

Perhaps what you told your friends has come true. Maybe employers came looking for you in droves, waving big money in your face and giving you a lovely choice from which to select the most advantageous deal. Or maybe there was one job offer that was right for you—all you needed was one.

There's a strong possibility, however, that you have discovered that as an unemployed job hunter you are nowhere near as desirable a piece of merchandise as "that hotshot from XYZ Corporation who's been giving our people fits in the marketplace." The telephone may not have rung at all. That was a rude awakening.

And when you started to call around, you were in for another shock. You dug out all of the business cards you saved from the last national convention. Some of the cards were from people who were very well oiled from three or more drinks in one of the hospitality suites. Some of the people made statements such as, "If you ever want to change jobs, I wish you'd do me a real big favor." Then the pause, punctuated by a wink. "Call me first!"

It is a very sobering situation. Many of those you called may not have remembered you. Most of those jovial people—the ones who slapped you on the back, flattered you, and made you believe that they'd love to steal you from your job—were simply talking to hear themselves talk or to build themselves up. Often these people were not even in hiring positions, or their positions may have changed since you met them.

But there was always the possibility that there was one straight shooter in the crowd. Because you couldn't afford to overlook that lonely one, you had to follow up on the whole bunch. Hopefully you uncovered that one good lead. Maybe you discovered that there wasn't even one. It's too bad that people bolster their fragile egos by making extravagant promises and bogus commitments.

BE REALISTIC

So after you've played out your string of big deals, reality must then be faced. The reality may be that no one out there needs you badly enough to stick out his or her neck for you.

If you're lucky, you just may walk in at the right time, when someone is really hurting for a person with your qualifications. If so, it's lucky for both parties. If not, you don't mean a thing to that company.

So what you have to do is roll up your sleeves and touch every base you can think of. Then, when you're convinced that there isn't another lead left in the world, you'd better wrack your brain and come up with dozens more. Remember the well-worn truism that the salesperson who makes the most calls usually gets the most sales? It works just as surely in the job-hunting business. So get moving and keep moving until you get what you're after.

WHAT ELSE CAN YOU DO?

Plenty. You merely think you've exhausted all approaches. Let me cite a personal example.

One time when I had been out of work for months and was verging on desperation, I was flying back to Los Angeles after an unsuccessful trip to Chicago. I was seated next to a man who had all the external earmarks of great success. He was well groomed, wore expensively tailored clothes, and had a Mark Cross cowhide briefcase on his lap. He started the conversation. Before long I learned he was a salesman, and a very successful one. After some prodding, I finally admitted to him that I was presently unemployed.

I guess sometimes when you figure you'll never see a certain person again, you tend to open up more than you would with even a close friend. So I found myself telling him my fear that I might never find another good job again. He gave me a look that indicated he couldn't understand that kind of negative thinking.

Then he pulled up the window shade on our 747 and turned out our overhead lights. We were circling Los Angeles on a clear evening. There seemed to be millions of twinkling lights visible in every direction. "See all those lights?" he asked me. "Well, think of them this way. For every light you see, there's a person down there who may be willing to buy what you're selling."

I looked at him. He was dead serious. "I never thought of it exactly that way," I told him. "What a wonderful way to look at things!"

He smiled. "That's the assumption I always operate on, and it's worked pretty well for me." He paused. "You know that old chestnut about whether the bottle is half-empty or half-full? Well, it may be a cliché, but it sure pays to look at the positive side of the situation."

We were getting ready to leave the plane. "Thank you," I told him. "It was very nice of you to listen to my problems."

He slapped me on the shoulder. "Hang in there, fella! One of those lights has your name on it."

That was just the lift I needed. As soon as I got home, I sat down with my wife, and we compiled a list of my strong and weak points. "What makes you think," she asked me, "that you have to limit yourself to advertising agencies or advertising departments or publications?"

"I guess it's what I know best," I said.

"Baloney!" she scoffed. "You're a writer, a salesman, an expediter, and a production expert. Let's try to think of some other businesses that need the same kinds of skills you've been developing all these years."

Starting with the A's and *Airlines,* we went through the entire alphabet and came up with about a dozen industries that might value the kind of attributes I had.

You can do the same thing, no matter what your duties were in your last job. Have you ever noticed how readily the top business executives move around and slide sideways into completely different situations? If not, try reading a few issues of *Forbes, Fortune, Business Week,* and other magazines of that sort, and you'll get the general idea.

Dr. Franklin Murphy, the present chairman of the board of The Times Mirror Company, parent corporation of the *Los Angeles Times,* moved to his job from the chancellorship of the University of California at Los Angeles. He replaced Albert Casey, who had left to become chairman of the board and president of American Airlines. Roy Ash left the presidency of Litton Industries to become head of the Office of Management and Budget under President Nixon. When he resigned from that post, he moved easily into the presidency of Addressograph-Multigraph. Paula Kent Meehan was an actress and then became chairwoman of the board of Redken Hair Products, a company she started. Dixie Lee Ray's working life has taken her from associate professor of zoology to a member of the Atomic Energy Commission to the governorship of Washington. Bess Myerson, New York City's Director of Consumer Affairs, is a former Miss America.

There are some positive steps you can and should take when you think you've exhausted all approaches toward that new job you need.

Check the Yellow Pages. Suppose you are an editor of a magazine and you've just lost your job. After you've tried everything else I've suggested up to this point, worn out every lead and avenue of approach, you should look in the Yellow Pages under *Publishing.*

You'll be surprised. You'll find several pages of possibilities. Some of the related categories would be *Publications—Editorial and Production Services; Publicity Services; Publishers—Book; Publishers—Directory and*

Guide; Publishers—Periodical; and *Publishers Repre-*
sentatives. You may end up with a basketful of possibilities. To save time, you can telephone a selected list, then
follow up the better prospects with letters and resumes.

Suppose you're a previously successful dress designer
who recently has had a run of hard luck. You'll find pages
of related businesses under the headings *Dress Forms;*
Dress Patterns; Dress Trimmings; Dress—Mfrs.; Dresses
—Retail; Dresses—Whsl.; Dressmakers; Dressmakers'
Supplies; and *Dressmaking Schools.* Get the idea?

Ride the range. That's exactly what I mean. Get into
your car and drive around the areas where businesses
such as yours are located or walk around the downtown
areas of your town or city. You may see a company that
strikes your fancy. If so, go inside and ask for the head of
the department you'd like to work for. As a general rule,
avoid the personnel department if you can. It's very unusual for a personnel manager to have the final say on any
job of importance. Sometimes you have to go through the
personnel department, but if you can bypass it, you'll be
better off.

Your timing just may be exactly right. Someone might
have just given notice that very day, or someone might be
sick. There hasn't been any time to go through channels
in an effort to get a replacement. If you do get a hearing,
ask for either full-time or part-time work. Stay loose and
surprise yourself.

Seek part-time or free-lance work. This can be one of
the best ways of demonstrating your value to a company
that doesn't think it needs someone full time. You may
be able to change the thinking on this. This option is
explored in chapter fifteen, "Tricks of the Job Hunter's
Trade."

Advertise yourself. In chapter six, we covered running your own ad in a newspaper, trade magazine, or *The*
Wall Street Journal. But don't stop there. Be original. For

example, did you know that you can buy a one-minute radio commercial on a local station in a large city for twenty-five dollars or less, depending on the time of day and the size of the audience? Now, wouldn't that be an attention-grabber? Why, you may even attract a newspaper reporter with an ad like that and get a lot of free publicity.

How about a billboard on the main thoroughfare near some of your most likely prospects? An outdoor advertising company would be happy to help you with it. You don't need any expensive art; just big, bold type will do.

Want to really go wild? How about a banner towed by a small plane or skywriting on the day of the big convention? Why not advertise on book matches and tip a bartender to pass them out in a strategically located bar?

One of the best stories I've ever heard about using ingenuity to land a job concerns Ernest Jones, now chairman of the board of D'Arcy-MacManus & Masius, the twelfth largest advertising agency in the world. When Mr. Jones was in college at the University of Michigan, he hit upon a scheme to attract the attention of executives from General Motors. He persuaded some of the students who sat in the section that spells out words on cards during halftime to do him a favor. Michigan was playing Ohio State at Ann Arbor. The traditional salute to the opponents during halftime was to spell "Bucks," the shortened version of Buckeyes, the nicknames of the Ohio State team. Mr. Jones persuaded some students to spell out an *I*, and to place it between the *U* and the *C*. So when the cheering section spelled out *BUICKS* that sunny afternoon, Ernie Jones was on his way. At least, that's the story I heard.

Here are a couple of other unique door-openers I've used with excellent results. Have the best delicatessen in town create the finest lean roast beef sandwich they can.

Have it wrapped beautifully and delivered by messenger to your prospect at about 4 PM. Enclose a short note, asking for five minutes of his or her time. It's hard to get a turndown on this one. I never did.

Or write your prospect a letter, enclosing a check for $10. Wait—this isn't a bribe! You start your letter by saying that you realize what a busy person the prospect is. And because you're so sure the prospect is going to like what you have to offer, you'd like to buy fifteen minutes of his or her time at the rate of $100,000 a year. (Figuring fifty weeks at 50 hours a week, not excessive for a hard-working executive, you come up with 2500 hours. That's $40 an hour.)

You're asking for just fifteen minutes for your ten dollars. Assure your prospect that even if time can't be spared to see you, you want him or her to cash the check and buy a lunch with it. Of course, you're pretty sure the prospect is not going to do that. Most likely, he or she will either see you or send back your check. In fact, even if you are seen, chances are that your check will be returned. The main point is that you have created a powerful impact with it.

It could be that some or all of these ideas are totally impractical for your situation. But what I'm really saying to you is to break the mold, dare to be original, and loosen up. If you do, it will say something about you to a prospective employer that transcends the sharpest resume or sample book ever put together.

Once you've started being creative, you're going to generate more and more ideas yourself. It's an automatic one-person brainstorming technique. You'll think up more ways to get to prospective employers than you'll have time to carry out. And, best of all, you'll start bubbling over with newly acquired self-confidence. After that, nothing or no one can stop you. Congratulations! You've lifted yourself out of the doldrums.

14

Never
Sell Yourself
Short

You must learn to cope with the vultures who try to beat down your salary requirements and thereby steal your services cheap. Just as your resistance to disease can be lowered by recent sicknesses, so can your resistance to ridiculously low salary offers be lowered by being out of work and out of leads. This is the time when the vultures come out of their nests and soar in circles above you.

I've never understood why any employer who was of sound mind would want to pull this kind of a dirty trick, no matter how unprincipled he or she might be. Nothing good could ever come of it. Let's say you were so desperate that you took a job at an extremely low salary. You'd probably prove to be worth a lot more than you were getting paid. So you'd resent the company and your boss more and more every day, until finally you found a job where you would be appreciated monetarily. Or it could happen that you'd be offended by the ridiculously low offer of a company, because you have convictions as to your true value. So you turned them down flat. The

137

company tries the same tactics on another person, and another, until the word gets around. Then the employers wonder why they can't even get people to apply.

If job hunters are willing to lower their standards extremely, they may soon be regarded as easy to get and thus be held in very little regard. I had three of these ridiculously low offers in the past. I'd like to share my reactions to each, and the results.

I had been out of work for almost a year. I soon had exhausted my job leads, since I was new in California and didn't know many people. It was 1962 and very hard to match my $30,000 salary as an advertising creative director. With 1962 prices and deflation, I had never had it so good, while I was working, or so bad, after the money started running out. I free-lanced a bit, but my lack of contacts prevented me from turning up very many assignments. Then I decided that I would get rich quick by writing a best-selling novel. I wrote the novel, then spent too many days watching the mailbox for that huge check that was undoubtedly in the mail. But it never came.

Finally, an acquaintance I'd known back in Chicago arranged an interview for me with the creative director of a very large advertising agency. "You'll have to be second banana to Bill," he cautioned me. "But they're good people to work for."

By now, I wasn't much worried about rank, title, or serial number. I just wanted to go back to work. So I called for an interview. Bill saw me and appeared to be very impressed with my background and accomplishments. I really had good feelings about this job, and thought it was all but wrapped up. "I want you to come in and meet some of the executives next week," he said. "Oh, did I tell you what the job pays?"

I told him he hadn't. "Fifteen thousand—that's to

start, of course." He was very apologetic. "I know it's far less than you were making, but this is really a fine company. And we'd like to have you aboard."

I thought fast. What did I have to lose? It was fifteen thousand more than I was taking in right then. "Okay— fifteen," I said, trying to look enthused.

We shook hands. "I'll be in touch with you by next week," Bill promised.

I stuck to the phone like glue all the next week. The only time I'd leave was if my wife was home and promised to stay within earshot of the telephone. It was a miserable time. I'd promised to take the whole family to Disneyland, but I couldn't take the chance of missing Bill's certain call. Of course, this was before I had the sense to get my answering service.

The phone rang plenty all week. But most of the calls were for my children, none from Bill. Not that week, the following week, nor the week after that.

Three weeks to the day, I called Bill. He was out of town. I left a message and waited again for his call. Nothing for another week. I phoned again. This time I talked with him. "Oh, yeah, Jerry. I should have told you. We changed our minds on that job. Instead of one body for fifteen, we hired two young writers at nine apiece."

"What made you change your mind?" I asked.

"The volume of work around here."

I was furious and had nothing to lose. "I don't understand you people," I said bitterly. "You offer a thirty-thousand-a-year man half the salary, and then you hire two rookies instead. Don't you know that I can write faster than either of them and do it right the first time?"

"Sure I know," he said, sounding embarrassed. "But it was a joint decision. I'm sorry."

The whole affair left a bad taste in my mouth. I mentioned it to a good friend who knew the ropes in our business. "He must have figured there was something wrong with you when you came down so fast," he told me. "You know and I know there isn't. And who knows what he would have done if you'd have said you couldn't take that kind of money."

I promised myself that it would never happen again. So I was ready for the next ridiculous offer, which came very soon thereafter. Again I was highly recommended by a friend from Chicago to the head of another agency, a successful west coast office of a large national firm. The managing director was bright, handsome, well dressed, smooth, and bottom-line oriented to the exclusion of any humanity. He was ruthless—let the troops fight over the raw meat, and the one who wins will be worth all the bloodshed. He looked me over, said he liked what he saw, and mentioned that my friend had spoken highly of me. He asked me to talk with his creative director and then come back to see him again.

I showed my proofbook and reel to his creative director, a man who appeared to be more than a little defensive. He attacked my work, commenting on commas and split infinitives. He was very picky. We were close to the same age. Perhaps he felt threatened by my track record. Whatever the case, we didn't hit it off very well.

Finally I was back in the managing director's office, relaxing in a huge leather chair, waiting for the bottom line. Now, mind you, he knew about my $30,000 salary too. "I checked you out with Curt. He thinks we could use you all right."

Curt was the creative director, and I was surprised. But I wasn't ready to turn handsprings yet. Something about this entire setup made me slightly uneasy. "If you can see your way clear to take $12,000, you can start next Monday," he said offhandedly.

I looked at his face to see if this was some kind of a joke. "You're kidding, aren't you?" I said. He looked very serious and shook his head slowly. "No, you're not kidding!"

He spread his hands in a gesture of helplessness. "It's all we have in the budget." Then he brightened up a bit. "But we're three miles closer to your home than your last job!"

I didn't dignify his offer with a reply. I simply picked up my proofbook and sample reel, packed them into the carrying case, and headed toward his office door. At the door, I turned. "Thanks for your time," I said. To his slight credit, he gave me a silly grin. The kind Disney's cartoon dog, Pluto, uses when he's just been caught in the act of raiding a cookie jar.

I've bumped into him at dozens of industry functions in the years since he made me that offer I could easily refuse. Up to this point, he hasn't yet been able to look me straight in the eye. I don't think he ever will be.

I ran across a number of other vultures before I found my next job. Some of their tactics were classics. One company convened three of their top executives to interview me together. I felt like a target in a shooting gallery. One by one, they grilled me about every job I'd ever had, the different kinds of accounts I'd worked on, and how I usually got my ideas. Before long, they managed to steer the conversation to their own accounts, casually asking me how I might handle this or that specific problem if I were to come aboard.

It was painfully obvious that they were picking my brain. They didn't even try to be subtle. But I was being interviewed for a job. It would have been rather difficult to clam up at that stage and still expect to be considered as a candidate. So I gave some noncommittal answers, putting them off with the valid reason that I'd prefer to

know more about the client's product before I could make
an intelligent recommendation.

About that time, the president looked at his watch.
"It's lunch time already," he said. "Could you come back
about one-thirty, and we can pick it up again?"

I didn't believe what I was hearing. Nothing was
mentioned about them having a lunch appointment.
They actually rode down in the same elevator with me,
headed toward the office building restaurant, and waved
with a "see you later." I spent the entire hour-and-a-half
walking, because I was too disgusted to be hungry. I
debated just forgetting the whole thing. But my sample
reel and proofbook were both stashed in the president's
office. So I had to go back.

One source of satisfaction was that I came back
fifteen minutes late, just to bolster my self-respect. "The
service is slow in the neighborhood," the executive vice-
president ventured. If he was fishing for some sort of an
excuse for my tardiness, he was going to have to bait his
hook again. I didn't acknowledge the comment.

I put up with the third degree for another hour and
closed my briefcase abruptly. "I guess we've covered
things pretty thoroughly," I said to all three of them.
"Now can we get down to cases?"

The president cleared his throat. "Let's discuss
money, and then we can wrap it all up."

"I thought the employment agent told you my salary
range," I said.

The treasurer spoke up. "Yes, he did. But we told him
we couldn't come close to that. He said maybe we ought
to talk anyhow."

This thing started to smell. "What do you mean by
not coming close?" I said. "I'm in the thirty-thousand
range, give or take a thousand." I felt I might as well get
it all out in the open. No one was going to pull another
twelve-grand deal on me.

"We were thinking in terms of about fifteen." He saw the look on my face. "That's starting out, of course. Later, and with Christmas bonuses and such, you could do quite well. You know, we have some very good fringe benefits."

I shook my head. "You're wasting my time, and I'm wasting yours. How can you even look me straight in the face with an offer like that? With my eighteen years' experience?"

The president spoke up. He had such an oily manner that I knew I couldn't work with this guy if he offered me fifty big ones. "We understand," he said. "You're a real heavyweight, don't get us wrong. But you have to look at it from our standpoint too. You'd be the last one hired, if you come with us. How can we offer you more money than some people who've been here for five or more years?"

I couldn't believe this clown! I shook my head as I stood. "Are you telling me that a clerk who's been working here for five years should get more money than a top creative man who's just walked in the door?" I picked up my samples. "I guess we're on totally different wavelengths, so we may as well stop right here!" I headed for the door. The three of them just sat there, watching me leave. Not a word was said.

I went right to a phone booth and called the employment agent who had sent me there. He was extremely apologetic. "I know it wasn't the right way," he said. "But I thought when they saw how good you are, they would come up on their offer." He never got another chance to do that to me, because he never saw me again. It was obvious that he depended on the buckshot technique to make his placements. He would send out as many bodies as he could muster on every job lead. His hope was that by sheer luck, one would land the job and earn him, the agent, a fat commission.

In addition to the situations I describe above, there

are other ploys to guard against. Watch out for the person who says, "I can't hire anyone for over X-thousand dollars without checking it out with New York [or wherever the home office happens to be]."

The person who says, "Things are very tight around town now. You'll be lucky to find a job open that pays more than X-thousand," hopes to push the panic button in your subconscious. He or she is the type who has an overblown idea of the value of the job being dangled in front of you.

And you may hear, "While we can't pay that much in straight salary, we almost always give an end-of-the-year bonus. It's based on our profits, and it has always been at least X-thousand dollars at your level. So if you could see your way clear to take five thousand less in salary, I can almost guarantee that you'll more than make it up by the end of the year." The way to handle this one is simply to ask for it in writing. End of interview.

I had this offer made to me a few years back, and I didn't buy it. Lucky for me. By the end of that year, the company had lost their single large account, worth a couple of million in billings. So they cut down from twelve people to three. So much for the big end-of-the-year bonus.

Summing up, there seems to be a certain type of person who is highly stimulated when he or she sees a person who appears to be having a rough time. I call these people vultures, because they figuratively fly in a circle above, waiting for the unfortunate person to fall. At that time, they'll light and feast on the carrion.

Most of the time, you can spot this type. You'll notice that the interview is being used to slip in little digs, to lord it over you because he or she occupies a comfortable slot and you have nothing. There's a discernible smugness that's stifling. You'll note the false heartiness with which fellow employees are greeted. The whole thing is just too goody-goody and phony to believe. When you encounter one of this type, don't waste any more time than is necessary. He or she hasn't the slightest desire to give you a helping hand and isn't even interested in how good you are. He or she really wants to steal you cheap and brag to the comptroller about keeping the costs down. Your best bet is to say courteously that you cannot go below your low limit and get out of there as fast as you can.

To be sure, there are situations when there truly is no money available for hiring an expensive employee. However, the interviewer will be obviously sincere in recognizing the circumstances and will not be trying to pull a fast one.

Vultures can strip you of some of your precious self-respect, while having nothing to offer in return. Learn how to spot them and avoid them at all costs. They're bad news!

15

Tricks of the Job Hunter's Trade

Here are some more hints that may help lead you to the full-time job that you seek.

AVOID PERSONNEL DEPARTMENTS

We've discussed this before, but it can't be over-emphasized. Usually, the main function of a personnel department is to screen out people. They rarely have clout with the people who do the actual hiring. So if you can bypass the personnel office you'll be miles ahead of the game.

TRY FOR PART-TIME ASSIGNMENTS

One of the better ways of getting a new job is to ask for a part-time assignment from everyone who interviews you. He or she probably needs help or you wouldn't be given an interview. If a replacement is being sought for someone who is leaving, there must be some work piling up. It may be a welcome relief if you offer to take on a part-time assignment in an area you're familiar with. Not only can you earn some much needed money, but you'll be giving the company a sample of how you work. And the people there won't have to commit themselves, which is fine for them.

Part-time work also gives you the chance to see the company at a close range, to observe the people you'd be working with if you were hired. You'll be less likely to make a bad mistake. Offering to work part-time says something about you—that you're willing to put yourself on the line and prove yourself without any strings attached. It has twice led me to full-time jobs. Make it a standard part of your routine to ask about part-time work at some time during every interview.

Another type of part-time assignment that helps you keep your hand in without committing yourself is registering with one of the agencies that handles temporary employment. Among them are Manpower Temporary Services, Kelly Girl, Greyhound Temporary Personnel Inc., and Accountants Temporary Personnel. There are pages in the Yellow Pages devoted exclusively to temporary-employment agencies. Part-time work will keep you informed about what's happening in your industry. You'll be given interesting assignments with various companies. And you'll make some money.

KNOW YOUR PROSPECT

We've discussed this in detail in chapter nine, under the heading "Learn About Your Interviewer." But it's worth taking another look, focusing on the prospect's needs.

One of the best ways to ensure success is to research

your target company thoroughly. Discover what it lacks, what its strong points are, and what it may be able to use to good advantage now. Then get the name of the person responsible for the area you have defined. Make an appointment to present him or her with your findings on how to correct or to institute something. You may virtually create a job for yourself this way, because you will have shown the company how to save money by using your services.

Hiring good people is an important part of a top executive's responsibilities, yet many executives feel uncertain in this area. You can make it possible for them to successfully complete what is not their most enjoyable task, enabling them to get back to their regular work.

KNOW YOURSELF

Nothing else is quite as important. Know what you have to sell and find out where it is in demand. Then think through how you can make a company believe that you are the one who can deliver what is needed. When you are sure of yourself, you'll find a job sooner rather than later.

DON'T BE A LONER

You are not alone. There are many others in the same fix—good people like yourself. Don't shun them under the mistaken impression that each is your competitor. You are as different as your fingerprints from all of them.

Get to know people you see at employment agencies, in the unemployment lines, and any other place where they're recognizable as job hunters. Each has probably been on one job interview where he or she wasn't properly qualified. Perhaps you could fill that spot. But you'll never know about it unless you communicate.

Jobless people have empathy, and most are willing to share leads. Perhaps you've been asked if you know a good industrial writer or a film producer while you've been after a completely different job. "We don't have a thing in your field," you might have been told. "But I could use a couple of good electronics engineers. You don't happen to know one, do you?" If you do know one and can send him or her around, you'll be doing both the engineer and the company a favor.

Unemployed people are a large but often voiceless minority, concealing their anguish because of an ill-considered desire to cover up. Don't be this way. There are many who would have great empathy for you and would help you if they knew about you and could help. Don't be ashamed to admit that you need help; don't go into a shell.

Job hunting is the world's loneliest business. You will have to fight off discouragement and loss of self-confidence and self-esteem. So keep telling yourself that you are not alone, that there are many, many people in the same boat—good people who are as willing to help you as you are to help them.

LOOK YOUR BEST

As a job hunter, you are essentially a salesperson, trying to sell yourself as a desirable employee. It's important to package yourself attractively. In the span of an interview, it is difficult enough for a potential employer to judge what fine qualities lie within you. Don't hinder him or her with your appearance.

Employers are looking for energy and fresh ideas. Make yourself look dynamic. Perhaps all it will take is a new suit or dress or a new attaché case. (If you buy something, buy quality—anything else is a waste of money.) Can you change your hairstyle to make yourself look more interesting?

However wrong it may be, many employers equate youth with creativity and energy. Would a color touch-up benefit you, or a hairpiece? If you're the one who always gets told "You don't look fifty!" or forty-five, or whatever, take advantage of it. If you can knock off three to five years, it may well influence your potential employer. Most employers are looking for long-term help. If you can be looked upon as a potential twenty-year employee instead of as a fifteen-year one, it may help. (You probably don't want to actually lie in writing, however; that can lead to problems with your social security benefits when you retire.)

To look younger, get plenty of sleep each night. Take it easy on alcohol and tobacco. Get a suntan, either outside or with a sunlamp. Take up jogging, swimming laps, or bicycling. Eat the proper foods. Being good to your body will naturally make you look younger and healthier. If a man, keeping your hair cut reasonably short, along with the aforementioned tinting, will minimize graying.

CHANGE YOUR OUTLOOK

When you've been out of work for a while, there's a tendency to develop a "what's-wrong-with-me?" attitude. There's nothing wrong with you. You simply haven't connected yet. But if you persist in telling yourself that there is something wrong, then there will be.

You must look on the bright side of the situation. You're still healthy. You still have your intelligence. A lot of other people who are not nearly as well qualified as you are seem to be doing okay. And so will you!

Change your attitude and image but not your integrity. There's a difference between putting a false face to the world and showing your best face. You are a very special person. Be sure that you look and act it. Don't be a defeatist.

LEARN TO RELAX

Tension is a great adversary of the job hunter. Tension builds and builds and eventually becomes self-perpetuating. False leads, wasted interviews, and turndowns tend to build up tension within you. If you're not careful, tension can do great harm.

Learn how to relax. The easiest and best single thing you can do is to practice deep breathing. Whenever you feel yourself getting tense, with an aching neck and bunching shoulder muscles, stop whatever you're doing. Breathe in as much air as you can, hold it for five seconds, and let it out slowly. Feels good, doesn't it? Now, do it again.

The wonderful thing about deep breathing is that you can do it anywhere, even in the reception room while waiting for that important interview.

Another effective relaxing exercise is to shrug your shoulders up as hard as you can, literally trying to touch your ears. Do it, then relax, going as limp as you can. This is an especially effective way to loosen tense shoulder muscles. It may look a bit strange in public, but there are dozens of opportunities to do it during the course of a day—while in an empty elevator; in a restroom stall; in the shower, at home; at the stoplight while driving; or on a bus or train. Do this one three times and feel the difference.

A third exercise can be done anywhere you're sitting. Just sit on the front edge of any chair or bench with your legs apart. Bend over, tucking your chin to your chest and exhaling as you go, and touch the floor with your hands. Straighten up and take a deep breath. Bend down again and exhale. Do the exercise three times.

These exercises work wonders relieving tension. I think of them every time I watch a pro golfer putting on the eighteenth green with thousands of dollars at stake or a pro tennis player serving for match point in a tie-breaker. If they would just take a few moments to do one of these exercises, it might make all the difference in the world in their performances.

16

How to Nurse
Your Capital

While you're taking home a regular paycheck, it is difficult to picture how it is to be winding down to where there just isn't any money left. Suddenly, you're faced with something cold, hard, and unyielding—the same outgo versus no income. Now inflation hits with a double whammy. The money stream has gone dry, but prices keep going up. It's enough to make a person panic.

I am not going to say, "Relax, it isn't as bad as it seems," because it is if your income contributed greatly to the support of your family. The world is a tough place when you're all out of money. You're a recently employed person, so you probably don't know the first thing about how to get welfare payments, food stamps, or free medical attention. There may come a time when you'll have to find out how to use these governmental services that you've been supporting all these years. Hopefully, the time will never come. Let's take first things first. These are my findings based on my own experience and that of people I interviewed. Use your judgment in deciding if you should see a financial counselor.

YOUR FIRST LINE OF DEFENSE

The best way to conserve your funds is to start right away, as soon as possible after you've been let go. Sit down with those you love and establish some priorities. Some things should go on as usual. You'll keep buying the necessities. But now is the best time to cut back on the luxuries, not when your bankbook is down to zero.

Lock Up Your Credit Cards. Have you ever noticed how much easier it is to spend money when you simply sign a credit-card slip, as compared to digging into your wallet or purse for those precious greenbacks? Put your department store and bank charge-cards in the safe-deposit box for the duration of your job hunt. The only exception should be a couple of oil company credit cards, which can be indispensable if you depend on your car for transportation.

Cut Out Discretionary Purchases. The dress that you "just have to have," the shotgun or fishing gear you've been eyeing, and the hot tub in the backyard are the things that aren't important enough to spend your money for at this point. Perhaps you've promised your son or daughter a certain item or a trip with friends. All your parental life, you've lived by the principle Never renege on a promise. Well, this is war. Talk with your youngster. You may find that the kid is made of sterner stuff than you thought possible. If not, it's time the youngster faced reality right along with you.

A new car, new washing machine, new refrigerator—all will have to wait. If your hand is forced when something breaks and cannot be repaired, scout around for a secondhand replacement. Read the classified ads, haunt the garage sales, or visit a flea market. Make do. Patch and improvise. Keep your capital as intact as you can.

Cut Out the Clubs. If you belong to a social club, golf or tennis club, or a yacht club, you know how much you're paying for dues and how the bar bills can add up over the course of a month. If you have equity in your membership, now may be a good time to put it up for sale. If not, see if it's possible to put your membership in cold storage for the duration of your job search. Perhaps you can go onto an inactive list, with an option for reinstatement. You may be able to come back to it sooner than you think. If you decide to try this, have a frank talk with the membership chairperson. He or she should be sympathetic. If not, perhaps you shouldn't be in that club after all.

YOUR SECOND LINE OF DEFENSE

If you haven't found a new job in four to six weeks, it's time to tighten your belt another notch. But a word of caution here. It's possible to economize *without making you and your family feel poor.* That would be self-defeating. If there's something you all enjoy—concerts, athletic events, movies, or whatever—consider that thing more of a necessity than a luxury. Keep on doing it until you simply cannot spare the cash. Hopefully, you'll be on a payroll before that day arrives.

The same goes for other things. If your children enjoy exchanging dinner invitations with their friends, let them continue doing so. Simply discourage last-minute invites, which wouldn't leave time to plan inexpensive yet nutritious meals for the guests.

Naturally, you won't want to economize on medical treatment. But it may be necessary to ask your doctor and dentist to wait for their money. If you've paid your bills on time in the past, they should be reasonable about it. Now let's talk about the ways you can cut down.

Cut Grocery Expenses. Here's the easiest place to save money without affecting your family's well-being. Cut down on beef and other red meats. Substitute chicken, cheese, eggs, fish, and beans. You'll be providing all the needed protein at a substantial savings, and any nutritionist will tell you that your family will feel better, too. When you entertain, serve hamburgers or spaghetti instead of expensive roasts. Your real friends won't think any the less of you. Others don't count.

Cut down on convenience foods such as frozen, processed, heat-and-serve dishes, and baking mixes. Instead, buy fresh foods in season, when they're cheapest and at their best. Bake from scratch. Look for the featured items shown in the largest type in the supermarket advertisements. They're usually the best bargains, whether in produce, meat and fish, or the canned goods and paper products sections.

Beware of phony bargains. Inspect cans, jars, and boxes to see how much is really inside and how much you're paying per ounce or pound. Just last week, in my supermarket, two-pound jars of peanut butter were selling for five cents more than the cost of two one-pound jars of the same brand. Even an item as prosaic as toilet tissue needs careful scrutiny. One brand selling for five cents less per four-pack of rolls looked suspiciously slender. I checked the total area listed. It was 228 square feet, compared with 282 square feet for the one that cost five cents more. At eighty-four cents versus eighty-nine cents, it was certainly no bargain.

If you live in a large city, find out where the public market is located. It's usually near where the produce trucks come in. Almost always you can buy produce, even meats and fish, plus groceries at prices ranging from one third to one half off.

Buy private label or store brands whenever possible. Nearly all large chains have their own brands. Some are even coming out with generic grocery products, with plain wrappers and no brand name. The package simply says "Detergent" or "Green Beans" or whatever. The products are all good buys, and the food items are all prepared by the chain selling them. You save a good percentage by choosing these products over a brand-name item or even a store brand.

Buy day-old baked goods at the bakery thrift shops that can be found in most cities. In many cases, these items are probably as fresh as the products on the supermarket shelves. You can save from twenty to forty percent on bread, rolls, cereals, health grains, and other products. To save gasoline, visit the store once a month and load up your freezer with bread.

Clip coupons from magazines and newspapers, and you can save dollars every week. Do your drug and cosmetics shopping at a cut-rate drug store. You'll save on name-brand merchandise and even more on goods with the store's own private label. Watch the papers for specials. Cut down on fancy cosmetics.

Cut Down on or Cut Out Liquor and Cigarettes. They're expensive and taxable to boot. If you can use this occasion to at least cut down on or even cut out liquor and/or cigarettes, you'll benefit physically as well as financially.

Be a Do-It-Yourselfer. Perhaps you've had a cleaning person come in once a week or a gardener to mow the lawn, water, and tend the growing things. Perhaps you call the plumber every time a toilet leaks or the electrician when a switch refuses to turn on the light. Start taking care of these things yourself.

Invest in a good home repair book, if you don't already own one. *The New York Times* publishes an excellent one, as does Time-Life Books. Your local bookstore probably has several, perhaps even in paperback. If you'd rather save the money, borrow a book from your library.

The thing that makes doing it yourself so attractive is that you're saving after-tax dollars. If, for instance, you were in the forty percent tax bracket while working, it means that if the plumber charged you $20 an hour, you would have to earn $33 gross in order to take home enough to pay the $20. If the bill came to $100, you'd need $165. This is why doing it yourself is so popular, even with people who have comfortable incomes. It's an excellent way to fight inflation. You may discover that it's fun to see an appliance that has been out of order suddenly start functioning again because you've fixed it. The books are well written and well illustrated to show how to handle most simple home repairs.

Conserve Energy. We should all be doing it, even if the object isn't our own economy. Turn off the lights when you're not in the room. The same goes for radios, television sets, and stereos. Get the entire family to cooperate. Keep the thermostat down to sixty-nine degrees in cold weather and sixty-four at night while you're sleeping. In hot weather, if you must use an air conditioner, set the thermostat to turn on at seventy-six instead of seventy-two. Run a room air conditioner as little as possible. Never run a dishwasher, clothes washer, or dryer unless you have a full load.

Don't use gasoline needlessly. Coordinate family errands into the minimum number of trips to the shopping center, church or synagogue, school, or playground. Ride the bus or a bicycle when possible. Buy self-service gas at the lowest possible price. If your car uses unleaded gasoline, you can save when you patronize an oil company such as Union 76. They offer a regular gas that's lead-free at regular gas prices. However, if you buy self-service gasoline, be sure to check the tires and under the hood. Keep tire pressure at recommended levels. Check the crankcase and the levels of the radiator and transmission fluid. If you can't do this, it makes more sense to pay more and get full service—if you burn a bearing or throw a rod due to a too-low oil level, it will cost you a lot more for repairs.

If you pay for water, you will want to economize on its use. Turn off faucets and fix any that drip. Put a brick in each toilet tank so less water will be used with each flush. Shave in a stoppered washbowl instead of under a running faucet. Don't wash or rinse dishes under a running faucet—fill a sink instead. You can save hundreds of gallons a month this way.

Wait on Clothing. You probably have much more clothing than you need. So declare a moratorium on buying clothes for any member of the family unless it's absolutely necessary. Last year's swimsuits will do just fine. If there's a sewing machine in the family, someone can make clothes.

When you must buy clothes, buy quality. Wait for the sales. There are post-Christmas, post-Easter, post-Fourth of July sales, Anniversary sales, Washington's Birthday sales, ad infinitum. It seems that the department stores find an excuse for a sale at least once a month. You'll save at least twenty percent, perhaps more.

Wait on Restaurants. The cost of restaurant meals has gone through the roof in the past ten years. If you take the whole family to any place more elegant than McDonald's, you can pay enough to buy a week's groceries. So forego dinners out. If you do eat out, it is a good idea to have your cocktails at home before you go to keep the tab at a more reasonable level.

Save on Odds and Ends. You may think there aren't any more places to cut corners and save. You're wrong. Every place you turn, there's a way to economize. How often have you spent a dime apiece for photocopies of letters or other material? Rediscover carbon paper and save. Do you buy magazines at the newsstand, or has your subscription to a favorite publication run out? Instead of buying or renewing, read periodicals at your library. Some magazines are even available for checking out. This can be a considerable saving.

One magazine that can be a big help during this period is *Money*. Try to find it at your library and read every issue. You'll pick up plenty of tips on saving and even some on job hunting.

When it's necessary to make long-distance phone calls, remember that it's cheaper before 8 AM and after 5 PM. If you live on the West Coast, you can phone before 8 AM and catch business people at their desks in the Midwest and the East. If you live in the East or the Midwest, you can phone after 5 PM with the same results in the mountain states or Far West. The rates go down again after 11 PM and are cheaper during the day on weekends.

These are some of the ways you can cut corners and save. You'll probably discover some other ways too. Making it a family game to use ingenuity will make economizing a lot more palatable.

CONDITION RED

If you haven't found your new job within three or four months, it may be time to take drastic measures. Cash is what keeps you and your family running, and your unemployment benefits, earnings of your spouse, and/or savings may not be enough. There should be few possessions that remain sacred at this stage, within the limits of sentiment, morale, and practicality.

Sell What You Can. Do you own any adult toys, such as a boat, camper, motor home, off-the-road cycle, gun collection, or a stamp or coin collection? Do you own a summer cottage, a ski lodge, or a vacation condominium? Do you have a big gas-guzzler of a car that could be sold or traded in for a sub-compact that delivers thirty-five or more miles per gallon on the highway? If so, now is the time to unload these luxuries. Do it before you absolutely have to. If you wait until the need is dire, some opportunist will smell the chance to steal them. Do it now, and you can still afford to say no when some ripoff artist offers you a ridiculously low price.

Do you have some antique jewelry or a nice diamond? Some experts have said recently that diamonds have never been priced higher than at this time. As what goes up usually comes down, this could be a fortuitous time to sell. Check on the value you will receive.

If you have two cars in the family, consider getting by with just one. You'll cut your driving and your insurance rates. You'll have smaller gasoline and repair bills. Your savings could mount up to a couple of hundred dollars a month. If your children are of driving age, find out if you can take them off your policy, since they probably won't have much opportunity to drive the one car in the family. That could cut your rates even more.

Consider the Old Homestead. The very last thing you want to touch is your home. It's too much of a psychological blow on top of all the other things that have clobbered you and your family. Resist it to the bitter end.

If you own your home and must pay a monthly mortgage installment that simply won't fit into your stripped-down budget, discuss your loan with your banker. Do not, repeat, do not wait until you are sent a warning that your loan payment is past due. Bankers are much more flexible than they used to be. Perhaps your banker can show you how to refinance your home, thus reducing the payments and stretching out the term.

Also consider renting out your home. You may be able to move into less expensive quarters and clear enough to pay your mortgage without dipping into your capital. Essentially, you would be keeping your home in cold storage until that happy day when you're back in a good job again. Be sure to have an attorney or a knowledgeable real estate agent assist you with the lease to prevent any bad mistakes.

If things really get bad, you may be forced to sell. The only silver lining is that real estate prices have never been higher. So you should make a good profit on the sale. The first $100,000 of capital gain on a private home is exempt from being taxed. This would be a once-in-a-lifetime exemption, but this may be the right time for you. If you move into less expensive quarters, either farther out of town or in a lower-rent district in the city, you should have generated a tidy sum to help you over the rough period.

If you live in an apartment, discuss your problem with your landlord. Pay as much as you can spare per month. Offer to pay interest on the unpaid balance if he or she will carry you for a while. If this doesn't work out, consider moving to a less expensive apartment. If you have children, try to stay in the same school district. You certainly wouldn't want to give your kids the added pressure of getting acclimated to a new school if you don't have to.

STOPGAP JOBS

Chances are that you'll never reach this point, any more than you'll have to sell your house. But it can happen. It may come as a shock to you to discover that jobs such as pumping gas, bagging groceries, or clerking in a store are not easy for an executive to land. Employers can see that you're overqualified, and they hesitate to train you, only to lose you as soon as you find a better job. Nevertheless, it only takes one job to put you on the payroll. And there are many such jobs out there, at wages that will buy a lot of groceries.

FOOD STAMPS AND WELFARE PAYMENTS

Let's talk about charity and about false pride. Would you label food stamps or welfare payments, if you reach the end of your financial rope, as charity? I wouldn't. After paying lots and lots of taxes for thirty-plus years, helping to provide welfare to those less fortunate and helping to subsidize food stamps, I feel I'm entitled to it. If I was at the point where my financial resources were drained and where I could prove my need, I would not hesitate for one minute to accept food stamps and/or welfare payments. This is exactly what these programs were originally established for, although they've been abused, of course. But you would be a most worthy cause. That goes for free medical treatment, too.

These programs are not easy to get enrolled in, unless one is a professional charity-taker, which you're not. You'll have to get used to long waits and short tempers. But if it's necessary, don't hesitate to apply. And don't let it get you down, because you are not going to stay down!

I live in California, so I checked with the Los Angeles County Public Social Services Department. A woman who asked to remain anonymous supplied the following information. She said that California's program is comparable to those of other states. In order to apply for welfare payments as an employable person, you must have no more than $1500 worth of personal property, including your car. Only $9 of this can be cash. Your real estate must have an assessed valuation of $7500 or less.

If you meet these conditions, you're close to flat broke, and you're eligible to apply for immediate welfare payments for you and your family, including enough to pay for food and shelter. You may also apply immediately for food stamps and medical services. In California, the name of the medical program is MediCal. Other states may call it MedicAid or some other name. But it's all essentially the same.

The chances are good that you'll never reach this point of desperation. But it's important that we cover all possibilities and prepare you for the worst that could possibly happen. If you're aware of all your options, you're in a much better position to survive. But in this land of plenty and of unlimited opportunity, the worst probably will never happen. You're going to do okay!

17

Take Care of Yourself

Right now, you're at the peak of your vulnerability. You can be much more easily hurt than under normal circumstances, so it's important for you to take good care of yourself in every way.

HOW TO COPE WITH LETDOWNS

Be prepared for the times when you will allow feelings of worthlessness to wash over you. Telling yourself that letdowns are inevitable will help you to cope with such feelings. Idleness tends to magnify any of the problems caused by being without a job. Try to keep busy with worthwhile things that you enjoy doing.

You are what you are. Let those you meet see the real you. Act naturally. If you appear stiff and tense, others will react to it and avoid you. No one wants to be associated with a loser. You are a winner, so be proud and confident. Keep in mind all of your past triumphs and accomplishments. If you find that your self-confidence is slipping, a good way to recharge it is to reread your resume. That should give you the boost you need.

Your self-image is all-important during these difficult days. In chapter sixteen, we discussed retrenchment and how to nurse your capital. It is a mistake to change your life-style drastically right away, and it may impede your job search. For now, do your best to live as normally as possible, but don't buy anything you don't really need, either.

Your business hours will be, or should be, filled with efforts to find your new job. We've discussed a number of ways to generate new leads after the first leads dwindle. Do not let discouragement slow you down nor self-pity cause you to abandon those tried-and-true methods.

Be prepared for the shock of rejection. You'll probably be interviewed a number of times before you hit the jackpot. That's what usually happens, so expect it. If you're ready, it won't take as much of a toll on you. If the job market happens to be bad, and if there aren't any jobs available that fit your background, you could be anyone, and you still wouldn't be able to land a job. There's so much involved—timing, luck, personal chemistry, and the state of your industry.

Tell yourself that it happens to the best of people. None of the four big job-erasers (mergers, new bosses, buy-outs, or shakeups of staff) is necessarily an adverse reflection on their unfortunate victims.

Even the president of the mighty Ford Motor Company saw the axe fall. During July 1978, after thirty-two years, Lee Iacocca, the fifty-four-year-old president, was fired abruptly by the Ford board of directors. Just as many people do, Mr. Iacocca probably saw it coming. Just a year after the office of the president was converted to a troika, one of Iacocca's underlings, Philip Caldwell, was brought up to equal authority. A couple of months before the firing, Caldwell was promoted so that he was over the president. After all the euphemistic statements had been released to the press, the real reason came out. Henry Ford II felt that Iacocca was too abrasive.

"I have been with the company for thirty-two years. What have I done wrong?" Iacocca asked.

Ford replied, "I just don't like you," to the man who had made a fortune for the company with the hugely successful introduction of the Mustang. So, as you can see, it does happen to the best of people.

Four months later Lee Iacocca bounced back as president of Chrysler Corporation. At this writing, he is working with great enthusiasm to bring this company back to profitability.

Another example is Richard Goodwin, former president of the Johns Manville Corporation. In October, 1976, he was preparing to report higher profits to a meeting of the board of directors the next day. He was fired abruptly, despite his fine record. According to inside sources, his sudden dismissal was undoubtedly caused by the resentment of the directors, who felt his style of management was too freewheeling.

Firings are constantly occurring in the sports world; coaches and managers with good records are suddenly let go. It's happening all around you!

You may feel lonely even though you're in the midst of your family and friends. This is a normal feeling. You may feel sad and withdrawn, mourning over the ending of a pattern of living you've fashioned over the years, over the loss of friends who have been part of that pattern, and over the destruction of a cherished routine.

When you throw yourself into a task with all your heart, there has to be a feeling of loss when that task is taken from you. It's somewhat akin to the death of a close friend or relative. If you mourn for a reasonable period of time, it should pass.

If it doesn't, and you give way to excessive brooding, it's time to seek outside help. You surely don't want your situation to destroy your personal life. Lack of money, loss of status, feelings of inadequacy, shock of rejection—all can converge on you simultaneously. It takes a strong person to withstand them for a sustained period.

What do I mean by getting outside help? Don't bottle it all up inside yourself—tell someone else. It can be your marriage partner or boyfriend or girlfriend, for who else should know you as well or care as much? It can be a wise and caring friend who can hear you out and help you see the positive side of the problem. It can be your minister, priest, or rabbi.

All of the above are untrained amateurs in the field of human emotions, however. If you find yourself bogged down in lengthy periods of depression that seem impossible to shake off, it may be time to get some professional help. Ask your doctor to recommend someone. If you can't afford it, be forthright. Many counselors charge according to the ability to pay. There are also free public clinics and family service organizations where top professionals donate their time, or group sessions where several people split the charges. No one need suffer for the lack of this kind of help if it is required.

KEEP YOUR GUARD UP

We've discussed your possible vulnerability at this particular stage of your job hunt. It is very important to fight against feeling too sorry for yourself. Don't develop a hangdog aura—there are plenty of people out there who would delight in aiming a swift kick at you when they thought no one was looking. These people can work their mischief in diverse ways. Some are liars and some are cheats. Others are prejudiced in every way possible. Still others delight in "shopping" for applicants because it makes them feel so snug and superior in their corporate cocoons.

I had one interviewer ask me to close his office door when it was already closed. I presume this was intended to unnerve me. It didn't, but it did disgust me. Another drugstore therapist played the silent game with me. After the initial introductions, he simply sat there and stared at me without uttering a single syllable. I suppose his game was to get me to start running off at the mouth to fill in the awkward silence. I fooled him and didn't. Of course, I didn't get the job either. But at that point, I didn't want it.

BE GOOD TO YOURSELF

Try to spend your leisure time as you normally would, difficult as it may seem at this time. Don't hibernate. Continue your social life within the limits of your resources. Get together with friends. Enjoy whatever you enjoy most, whether it be music, movies, theater, or sporting events.

While it's important to put in regular office hours during your job search, it's also important to treat your weekends as though they really were weekends. Try to do your regular weekend things rather than pore over your resume and letters. During the week, days and evenings both if necessary, you can and should work hard at your job search. But you need relaxation to keep a positive attitude and forget your problems. Try to get away now and then for the weekend—to a resort, the shore, or the mountains. You'll be the better for it when you come back refreshed, ready to attack the problem with renewed vigor.

WIVES NEED TLC, TOO

This is directed solely to husbands of women who don't have outside jobs. You're probably all wrapped up in yourself and your problem, which is normal. You're the provider, and suddenly you're not providing. You're worried sick about the whole thing.

But have you, for a moment, considered that your wife may be going through an even worse experience? You're probably getting a full quota of sympathy from your friends and former compatriots. It may not help to pay the bills, but it certainly helps to lift your spirits.

But your wife is stuck at home, and she isn't getting one ounce of that outpouring of sympathy. On the contrary, she may be experiencing feelings of panic. When the mail comes, she is the one who sees the bills first. She knows what you have poured into your job, and it hurts her very much to discover that you were not really appreciated. Even if there's an understandable reason, such as a merger or a cutdown on a sales force, it still hurts.

She should be able to confide in someone, but she may believe it wouldn't be wise. Encourage her to get it off her chest. She probably doesn't want to burden you. Reassure her that it is a joint problem, one you must face together. Encourage her to confide in a dear friend, too. An objective viewpoint is necessary in order to place a problem in its proper perspective.

IT'S USUALLY DARKEST
BEFORE THE DAWN

We all know about Murphy's Law: If something can possibly go wrong, it will. But there's an opposite side to that. Things tend to improve eventually, even if it's because they can't get much worse. Think how frustrating it is for a boxer to give up after a bruising battle, only to have his opponent admit that he, too, was about ready to throw in the towel. Baseball players know that the game is never over until that last out in the ninth inning. Quarterbacks in the National Football League find their juices flow freely after the two-minute warning.

You may say, "Okay, so it works in sports. But this is the cold, cruel world, and I cannot buy these storybook endings."

And I reply, "How do you know who, at this very moment, is hurting somewhere for the lack of a person like you? How do you know the phone won't ring or the jackpot letter won't arrive today?"

If you still feel down about it, remember that the alternative to being optimistic is being a quitter. And no one wants to hire a quitter.

18

When You Get an Offer

When is an offer not an offer? When it's not in writing. Never stop looking; never rest on your laurels. You haven't been hired until you either sign a contract or actually start work. If you can get a letter of intent, do so. It really can help. The annals of business history are filled with tales of people getting hired, then quitting their old jobs only to discover that the people who hired them have just been fired themselves. If you have your job offer down on paper, you have a better chance of holding a company to its bargain.

I asked a nationally known advertising and communications attorney, Myron D. Emery, for his advice on how important it is to get it in writing. He stated, "In any employment situation, it is imperative to get your agreement in writing." Enough said.

SHOULD YOU GRAB THE FIRST OFFER?

You've been out of work for a long stretch. You've

almost forgotten how it feels to get a good paycheck. Suddenly, someone makes you an offer. Is there any doubt that you'll accept? There should be.

Sure it's tempting, because you've been out so long. But keep your standards high. It's your life. Resist the blandishments of any unscrupulous placement person who may be more interested in the fee than in your welfare. Being in a job where you're unhappy can be worse than being unemployed.

If you simply do not like the first job offer you get, should you take it just to pay the bills? Not if you can help it—life is too short. If you are one to commit yourself wholeheartedly to an assignment, you'd be wasting your energies on something you don't believe in. In deciding whether or not a job is right for you, more often than not, you'll have a gut feeling about what you should do. Trust that feeling. If you do take the job, and it doesn't seem right, trust your feelings then, too. Make a clean break before you've invested too much of yourself in it.

Don't panic. Don't say to yourself, "What's wrong with me? Can't I ever be satisfied?" Many people imprison themselves in unhappy situations because they don't want to be thought of as quitters. It's far better to be honest with yourself and admit it won't work than to stick with a job you can't tolerate. You won't be doing anyone any good.

Sooner or later, other offers are bound to start coming in. How would you feel if you took a job, perhaps conceding on salary and compromising on job satisfaction and future prospects, and the very next week, something perfect came along? You'd hesitate to jump, but then you probably would. After all, you have to look out for yourself.

A friend was faced with this identical decision. He told me that he had about given up hope that he was going to land the available job he knew he was perfect for. Let's call it Job A. Then he got an offer from a smaller company and accepted. We'll call this one Job B.

Two weeks later, he was finally offered Job A, his dream job. Being an honest and considerate person, he had an agonizing decision to make. After much soul-searching, he finally decided to quit Job B, after only two weeks on the job, and take the one he really wanted.

He told me that his resignation meeting with his employer at Job B was one of the longest, most traumatic half-hours of his life. They were furious and rightly so. The two weeks had been a costly period of indoctrination, and now they'd have to start over. But my friend bit the bullet, quit, and now he's happy in Job A.

Should he have waited a while longer for an offer on Job A? I don't think so. It might never have been offered to him. And Job B was a good job, too. So he did the right thing for himself in making both decisions.

WHAT ABOUT RELOCATING?

Relocating depends on your situation. Some careers bloom better in specific geographic locales. Be flexible and go where the action is in your chosen field. If you're in the oil business, it can be Texas, Oklahoma, Louisiana, or California. If you're an advertising or publishing person, you may have better luck in one of the large communications centers, such as New York, Chicago, Detroit, Los Angeles, San Francisco, or Houston. Unless you're anchored to a locale for personal reasons, geographic flexibility will increase your chance of landing that job.

WHAT ABOUT OVERSEAS?

Accepting an offer of a foreign assignment depends on your personal situation, the attractiveness of the job, and where in the world it's located. If your family has grown up, if you haven't yet started one, or if your children are unusually adaptable, why not go? Why not see a foreign country?

Do your homework before you decide. Check the tax situation. Check the cost of living in the country you are considering, how the currency stacks up with the dollar, and what types of bonuses, cost-of-living inducements, and financial help the company offers to Americans going abroad. How long must you agree to stay? What kind of a deal will you get? Will you be placed in a comparable job with the company after your contract expires and you return to the United States? Get it all in writing.

Consider the negatives. If you don't like the job, you may be stuck with it. If you don't like your fellow workers, you're stuck with them. Your family may not adapt. The alien culture may not be pleasing to you. Business may be conducted much differently from what you are used to.

Weigh the positives against those negatives. You'll be going on an adventure, the likes of which most people never get a chance to experience. You'll travel and get paid for it. You and your family will expand your horizons, learn different customs, and make friends you never would have met under normal circumstances. The entire proposition is a trade-off, and only you can decide whether or not the scales balance in favor of accepting the job.

THE PROS AND CONS
OF A CAREER CHANGE

Be wary of that tired cliché, "One of these days I'm going to chuck it all and get out of this rat race." I've heard teachers say it and become advertising copywriters. I've heard advertising copywriters say it and become teachers. It all depends on where you are now; the other person's situation invariably looks more attractive.

One question you should ask yourself is if there is any way you can do better financially than in the business you've spent all those years learning. If your answer is yes, then you may wish to consider the change. But the odds are that you'd be starting over from square one, competing with kids fresh out of college who can afford to take lower salaries.

If, however, you've pursued a lifelong hobby, and you see an opportunity to make it your vocation, that's different. Stamp collectors often go into the stamp business. I know a sales manager whose hobby was binding rare books. He quit his job and turned his hobby into a business. Now he makes more money than he ever did on salary, and he loves every minute of it. I know an artist who decided to open a tack shop. He and his wife love horses and riding. They're making a big success of it and having more fun than ever before. Of course, many more don't make it in their own businesses, even if they were successful hobbyists. It's a chance one has to take after a careful investigation of the pros and cons.

THE MID-LIFE CAREER CHANGE

Recently, the national magazines have massaged this subject relentlessly. There are stories about people who chuck their careers and go in an entirely new direction. Some follow their hobbies, as we've just discussed. Others want to change careers, but they have to go back to college to prepare themselves. Then there are those who want to get out of what they're doing now, but they aren't sure what they're fit to do.

I was once in that last category. I imagined that I would make a good salesman. I fantasized that I could become very rich as a star salesman if I'd only give myself the chance. After all, I'd been selling all sorts of products, from automobiles to cake mix, through magazine, newspaper, television, and radio advertising for all those years.

I signed up for a series of tests at the UCLA counseling department. It cost me a couple of hundred dollars to discover that I wasn't cut out to be a salesman, after all. I was given personality tests, aptitude tests, social tests, and an IQ test, all focused on the attributes that I possessed and where they could best be utilized.

What I did discover was that I'd make a good advertising copywriter, which I was and still am, or a good small-town newspaper editor.

Any good psychological-testing firm or college counseling service can give you a series of tests such as the ones I took and interpret them for you. If you are dissatisfied with your present occupation and figure that as long as you're looking around, maybe a career change is indicated, it will be money well spent. You may even be surprised to discover, as I did, that you're in the field you're best suited for. Conversely, an artist I know took the tests and found out that he would make a better insurance salesman. He switched careers and is doing very well!

WHAT ABOUT A BUSINESS OF YOUR OWN?

One of the first things that crosses an unemployed person's mind is that perhaps now is the time to start his or her own business. Be careful. If being an entrepreneur is your cup of tea, how come you waited so long? Born risk-takers usually start early; most would never consider working for anyone else. So ask yourself if this is a second choice, a panic move, or a face-saving maneuver so you won't have to go out and look for a job.

It may be that you can start your own business doing exactly what you've been doing for employers all your life. This way you can reap the fruits of your own labor. If you can swing it, and if you're the type who can endure hardship, sacrifices, and rebuffs until you get established, go to it. But don't use it as an escape hatch.

If you are so inclined, there are dozens of books in your library that will give you some of the guidance you'll need to get started. One of the best is *You, Inc.*, by Peter Weaver, a syndicated columnist whose column, "Mind Your Money" appears in many newspapers. It also pays to contact the nearest Small Business Administration office and find out what help you can get there. In addition to making loans available to qualifying applicants, the Small Business Administration conducts seminars where successful businesspeople share their know-how with newcomers. People are starting new businesses every day. Some succeed. More fail. Be sure you're ready to make sacrifices and risk going broke before you commit yourself to starting your own business.

19

Happy Days
Are Here Again!

After all the false starts, the blind alleys, and the disappointments, it happens. A letter arrives. Or maybe the phone rings and a voice asks, "Are you still interested in the opening we discussed last week?"

You try not to sound too eager. "Yes, I am." No more, no less. This is no time to be effusive.

Your prospective employer sounds pleased. "Good! Can you come in tomorrow morning? We'd like you to meet a few of the department heads. Then you and I can nail down your salary and some other details."

Your heart starts beating a bit faster. You repress the impulse to let out a war whoop. You make an appointment. You've already given your bottom salary, so it will be merely a matter of pinpointing the exact figure.

You spend some time that evening mentally rehearsing how you'll handle yourself the following morning. This is no time to be too relaxed. A blunder can still take you out of the running. The important thing is to be yourself.

HOW TO CONDUCT NEGOTIATIONS

The next morning's meeting is a very important one. Most of the details you discuss and agree upon will stay with you throughout your employment with the company, so consider each point carefully. If there is anything that you're doubtful about, it is wise to say, "May I sleep on it and phone you tomorrow?" This will give you time to discuss it with a trusted friend or with your accountant or attorney.

Should you ask for a contract? Only you can answer that. If a person is being lured from a fine job, he or she is in the driver's seat and can call the shots. But you've been out of work, and they know it. Don't ask for a contract unless you're prepared to be turned down. If they suggest one, that's different. In that case, have your attorney go over the contract carefully before you sign it.

Even if there's no contract, you should still get your agreement in writing, as discussed in chapter eighteen. It should include your job description, the person you will be reporting to, and your salary. If any promises are being made of benefits based on future performance, get those promises in writing, too. That's in case the person who makes the promises to you should happen to leave the company. If it was just a verbal promise, you might have a lot of trouble proving it was ever made.

Some people are reluctant to ask for what they want. They have the misguided notion that one must prove himself or herself before making demands. That's nonsense. When you start work, your employer is every bit as anxious to please you as you are to please him or her.

You may feel that in asking for what you want you

will appear more concerned over the "gimme's" than with what you can do for them. Worry not. You wouldn't have been hired if you hadn't sold yourself as valuable to them. A top executive once told me, "Remember, if they're willing to pay you thirty or forty thousand, they must be very sure they can make at least a hundred thousand from your efforts." It's true. A business is not a charitable organization.

How you ask is important. You may say, for example, "I'm very anxious to get started and help this company set new earnings records. But in order to give the job my total energy and dedication, I can't be distracted by any personal wants, likes, or dislikes. So I'd like to get all the details of my employment ironed out first thing. Then I'll be able to attack my job with an uncluttered mind."

This should pave the way for a discussion of salary, vacation time (including any extra time off you may need), whether or not you'll have a company car, details of your expense allowances, and any other perks you feel entitled to. This is the time to ask; there probably will never be a better opportunity.

"CAN YOU START MONDAY?"

Sweet music! You shake hands on it. Then you're introduced to a few people you'll be working with. They seem nice, and you try to remember their names and duties. But things are in a sort of rosy haze. Finally, you leave and head for the nearest telephone to break the good news to your spouse or the person closest to you.

The chances are good that between now and next Monday, you'll be doing a bit of celebrating—and about time. The road back has meant a rough, tense ride. Now you can lean back and savor your successful completion of a hazardous journey. So share the joy with those you asked to share your burden. Make it a family celebration. Everyone deserves it.

REMEMBER YOUR FRIENDS

Recall the dismal days when nothing seemed to go right and how appreciative you were of those who stood by you with encouragement and solid assistance? They were your true friends. They suffered your despair and bolstered your sagging ego. Now they should be able to share your joy.

Human nature being what it is, some successful job hunters suffer a complete lapse of memory once they've found their new jobs. They completely forget about all the help they received during the long, dreary months of their search. Ironically, these are often the very same people who were complaining the most about some of their fair-weather friends.

Don't be that way. Get the good news to your friends right away, before you do anything else. It's the very least you can do for them.

YOUR FIRST WEEK

This can be a critical time for you, the time when first impressions are made. Be yourself, be friendly, and be careful. It's natural for you to feel nervous, but try not to let it show.

Do your job quietly and well. Ask questions if you don't know all the answers. People enjoy being asked. And it shows you're not too proud to admit you don't know everything.

Watch out for overly friendly people who try to overwhelm you with attention the first day. They may be of the type who go from one new employee to another.

Sometimes you can spot this type of person from the way he or she confides in you immediately or wants to discuss personalities of some of the people you'll be working with. Fend these people off, courteously but firmly. Once it becomes apparent that you're not having any of their gossip, they'll move on to the next newcomer.

Usually, you can expect to be given a large batch of papers, forms, and applications to fill out the first day. Some of these will probably be for fringe benefits such as health insurance, life insurance, profit-sharing plans or pension plans, stock plans, credit unions, special deductions, and so on. You probably won't have time to fill out all of them because you'll be getting introduced to some of your colleagues, getting the proper supplies for carrying out your duties, and perhaps even getting an early job assignment. But no matter how busy you are, don't rush on these important papers. Read everything carefully and ask questions if you're not sure about something. If you need more time to complete them, ask for an extra day.

STAY OUT OF MENTAL FOXHOLES

The late Robert Ruark, noted columnist and novelist, once wrote a powerful column commenting on the compulsion of many Americans to build bomb shelters during the days after World War II. Ruark wrote that he would not live in a mental foxhole for the rest of his life. The greatest tragedy then, he said, would be if the bomb didn't fall. All those years would have been wasted living in fear.

You can draw the same analogy about fearing that you may lose this new job you've just landed. Sure, you've had a rough time of it. And you'd hate to go through the job-hunting ordeal again. But if you allow this kind of fear to bother you, you'll be cringing in your own mental foxhole. It will affect your work and your life. Don't let it. It's not worth it.

Tell yourself that nothing lasts forever. Something may happen to this new job, or you may get a better offer and leave. Whatever the circumstances, it will do you no good at all to worry about something that may never happen.

It is better to act and feel secure because you're doing such a good job. Your attitude will be catching.

LOOK OUT FOR YOURSELF

The flip side of the mental foxhole should be the realistic manner in which you handle yourself. Always give as much as you receive, perhaps more. But be careful of committing yourself heart and mind, body and soul. American business, with a few scattered exceptions, is totally geared to the bottom line, the almighty profit-and-loss statement. If, in the opinion of your supervisors, you're not making money for the company, out you will go.

Beware of blind or misplaced loyalty. If you are loyal to yourself, you'll do well for the company, too. And you are less likely to be shocked to your soles or feel betrayed if you should happen to be lopped off the roster.

It is also a good idea to start your own retirement program. Although Uncle Sam keeps tightening pension laws to protect workers, it's still a one-sided situation. The company sets up its own pension plan and always calls the shots. You can still get hurt.

Buy an hour or two of a good financial advisor's time. Tell him or her where you want to be financially by retirement time. With a plan of your own, Social Security payments, and any pension you may have coming from your company, you'll be in much better shape than if you put your entire trust in a benevolent company that can suddenly change its stripes.

It is a good idea to put a fixed percentage of your take-home pay into some kind of savings. Start first with a savings account until you've accumulated the equivalent of six months' take-home pay. Then get some life insurance that's yours alone, not some group policy that expires the very day you go off the payroll. You can get the cheapest kind of declining term insurance, enough to protect your family. Put some of your money into inflation protection, which could mean mutual funds, real estate, or good common stocks.

YOU'RE A DIFFERENT PERSON NOW

Think back to the day you left your last job. Now look at yourself. In retrospect, you're not the same person at all. Like a fine steel blade, you've been tempered by the fires of adversity. You're stronger and more honest with yourself. You've been down in the depths of despair, yet you've survived and grown. Now you're back near the top, but on a much firmer footing than ever before. You like yourself more, and you've developed an inner core of steel. No one can possibly hurt you as much again.

IT CAN HAPPEN AGAIN

Yes, it can. But if it does, it won't hurt the same way. You know how to handle yourself and your situation. Your family, too, has traveled the long trail and grown stronger. All this strength and confidence is one of your greatest assets. Ironically, it's the best assurance that it won't happen again.

Epilogue:
How to Avoid
Getting Fired

The thrust of this book is how to survive getting fired, which generally means how to find another job hopefully as good as the one you left. By now you may already have traveled the long journey back to the world of pay-days, business lunches, and everyday problems.

Once you are in a new job, however, a feeling of insecurity may tend to crop up. "How long will this one last?" you may find yourself wondering. "What if we lose our biggest customer?" Or "What if someday, when they need a hot idea fast, my mind won't function? What if everything simply goes blank?"

It's important at this point to discuss the subject of avoiding getting fired. There are no guarantees, as you know. It happens to the best of us. However, there are a few principles and warnings to heed that can help you keep your job. In fact, if you follow this advice, you should be that much more marketable even if the axe does fall.

BE THERE WITH A SOLUTION

The large firm I was with in Chicago displayed a sign in the conference room where we met frequently to hammer out recommendations for our clients' advertising campaigns. The sign read, "Are you here with a solution, or are you part of the problem?"

You would be amazed how that sign cut down on the hot air and needless competition. It affirmed management's no-nonsense dedication to getting the job done. We started doing our editing before the meetings, instead of bringing in raw ideas that needed more thought.

How can you be there with a solution? Simple. Whenever you are ready to present some work or to turn it over to your boss, stop for a while. Tell yourself that perhaps you're not quite ready yet. Then play the devil's advocate —see how many holes you can punch in your own work. Stand back and look at it as others will see it. Ask questions about it, and see if you can answer them. Then make all needed corrections until your work is infinitely better than you ever thought it could be. Now when you present it, you have a much better chance of coming up with a solution that works.

MAKE YOURSELF INDISPENSABLE

I once knew a very insecure man who kept such jumbled files that he was sure no one else could find anything. That was his way of being indispensable. But it didn't work; he was fired anyway. His replacement decided to start fresh. She threw away all the files, instead of trying to make sense out of it all. She's still with that company and moving ahead fast. She sensed correctly that anything buried that deeply could hardly have been vital to the job.

What do I mean by being indispensable? It's that

unique aura of reliability, trustworthiness, and skill that
makes other people come to you when there's a particularly tough problem to solve.

You've seen people like this. Invariably, everyone
around them competes for their time or attention. An
indispensable person is one of whom it is often said, "I
wish I had a dozen like him [or her]. We'd get our work
out in half the time!"

This quality of indispensability is often hard to define. In my judgment, it was never expressed better than
in an advertisement published in *The New York Times*
back in 1920. The ad has been reprinted many times in
advertising books.

BROWN'S JOB*

Brown is gone, and many men in the trade are wondering who is going to get Brown's job.

There has been considerable speculation about this.
Brown's job was reputed to be a good job. Brown's
former employers, wise, gray-eyed men, have had to
sit still and repress amazement, as they listened to
bright, ambitious young men and dignified old ones
seriously apply for Brown's job.

Brown had a big chair and a wide, flat-topped desk
covered with a sheet of glass. Under the glass was a
map of the United States. Brown had a salary of
thirty thousand dollars a year. And twice a year
Brown made a "trip to the coast" and called on
every one of the firm's distributors.

He never tried to sell anything. Brown wasn't exactly in the sales department. He visited with the

---

* Reprinted with the permission of Batten, Barton, Durstine &
Osborn, Inc.

distributors, called on a few dealers, once in a while made a little talk to a bunch of salesmen. Back at the office he answered most of the important complaints, although Brown's job wasn't to handle complaints.

Brown wasn't in the credit department either, but vital questions of credit usually got to Brown, somehow or other, and Brown would smoke and talk and tell a joke, and untwist his telephone cord and tell the credit manager what to do.

Whenever Mr. Wythe, the impulsive little president, working like a beaver, would pick up a bunch of papers and peer into a particularly troublesome and messy subject, he had a way of saying, "What does Brown say? What does Brown say? What the hell does Brown say?—Well, why don't you do it, then?"

And *that* was disposed.

Or when there was a difficulty that required quick action and lots of it, together with tact and lots of that, Mr. Wythe would say, "Brown, you handle that."

And then one day, the directors met unofficially and decided to fire the superintendent of No. 2 Mill. Brown didn't hear of this until the day after the letter had gone. "What do you think of it, Brown?" asked Mr. Wythe. Brown said, "That's all right. The letter won't be delivered until tomorrow morning, and I'll get him on the wire and have him start East tonight. Then I'll have his stenographer send the letter back here and I'll destroy it before he sees it."

The others agreed, "That's the thing to do."

Brown knew the business he was in. He knew the men he worked with. He had a whole lot of sense, which he apparently used without consciously summoning his judgment to his assistance. He seemed to think good sense.

Brown is gone, and men are now applying for Brown's job. Others are asking who is going to get Brown's job—bright, ambitious young men, dignified older men.

Men who are not the son of Brown's mother, nor the husband of Brown's wife, nor the product of Brown's childhood—men who never suffered Brown's sorrows nor felt his joys, men who never loved the things that Brown loved nor feared the things he feared—are asking for Brown's job.

Don't they know that Brown's chair and his desk, with the map under the glass top, and his pay envelope are not Brown's job? Don't they know that they might as well apply to the Methodist Church for John Wesley's job? Brown's former employers know it. Brown's job is where Brown is.

KNOW WHEN TO SIT TIGHT

You may find yourself feeling that your job is intolerable. You tell yourself that if you have to spend another month there, you'll go crazy. You've just got to get out of there at all costs.

It could be that your imagination is running away with you. Companies are made up of people, and people are pretty much the same everywhere. Certainly there are cases where someone over you could make life miserable for you. But these cases are in the minority.

Years ago, a dear business friend wrote me an anguished letter. He had left what he thought was an unbearable job, only to land in one he felt was equally unbearable. He wanted to quit once more. But he hesitated because he didn't want to be thought of as a job-hopper.

I answered his letter with what I thought was good advice, and he stayed put. Then he showed my letter to the editor of *Art Direction* magazine, who published it with my permission. I'd like to repeat it here, for it makes the point well.

DEAR BUD,*

Thanks for your letter. I've been wondering how you were getting along in your new job. You say you hate to sound like a malcontent, but you're still unhappy. But for different reasons this time.

Well, let's face it, you were due to make your last move. When you've tried everything and then can't settle your differences with the guy who owns the business, it's time to leave. So you left.

You like the people fine in your new agency. But you complain that they hired you to improve the visuals on that food account, and now they won't let you do it. You say you're supposed to keep laying out that same tired stuff they've always bought. And finally you say you wouldn't have taken the job if you'd known it would turn out this way. And you want to know what I think.

Here it is. The key words in your letter are "I wouldn't have taken the job if I'd known." I'll bet everybody in our business has said that at least once, and meant it.

---

* Reprinted with the permission of *Art Direction* magazine

But can you ever really *know* without first trying out the job? I don't think it's possible. When you're considering changing jobs, you tend to minimize any possible drawback of the new opening, and to inflate any apparent advantage. But, let's face it, nobody can predict the strange chemical reaction that makes one person a pleasure to work with, and another one impossible. You just can't foresee how you'll get along with your fellow workers—or the client—until you've tried it out. Nor can you tell in advance whether or not you'll gain satisfaction from your efforts.

Does this sound hopeless? Does it doom you to a Don Juan-like business life, hopping from one job to another until you find the one perfect spot (which exists only in your dreams)? Not necessarily. Because, when you clear away the hopes and disappointments, one solid fact stands out: No matter how attractive the new offer appears, and how unbearable your present job may seem, *you merely exchange one set of problems for another.*

Once you accept this fact of business life, it could help you make a wise decision next time. (And, from your letter, that may be soon.) Simply ask yourself these questions:

1. Are my present problems unbearable?
2. Do I think the problems I'll encounter in the new job will be easier to live with?

If your answer to each is "yes," you've already made up your mind. But if you find yourself answering either question with "I'm not sure," then better give yourself a few more months in your present job. The situation might improve faster than you think right now. Remember, proving yourself to strangers over and over again can be mighty wearing on the nervous system. For, sure as death and taxes, you'll find a brand new set of problems waiting for you at your next job. Worse yet, maybe even the same old ones!

Sincerely,
Jerry

Even the best of jobs can get on your nerves. That's when you may start looking for greener pastures. A former boss of mine, when asked when a person should change jobs, replied, "When it stops being fun coming to work in the morning."

On the surface, that answer makes a certain kind of sense. Everyone ought to enjoy the work he or she does. But if we all took this literally, we'd have the longest game of musical chairs this country ever saw. It isn't always fun; sometimes you can go weeks without it being fun!

If you have considered all sides of the question, and you still feel that you want out of your job, start looking for a new job right away. Try to keep your feelings under control, however. If your dislike of your job and/or the people at your job begins to show, you could find yourself out of the job before you're ready to leave.

BE WORTH MORE THAN YOU'RE PAID

Every payday, give your boss the supreme joy of realizing that he or she has bought a real bargain. Then you'll feel as secure as any person in any job.